Ferns & Allies
of the North Woods

By Joe Walewski

Ferns & Allies
of the North Woods

By Joe Walewski

Kollath+Stensaas
PUBLISHING

Kollath+Stensaas Publishing
394 Lake Avenue South, Suite 406
Duluth, MN 55802
Office: 218.727.1731
Orders: 1.800.678.7006 (Adventure Keen Distributors)
info@kollathstensaas.com
www.kollathstensaas.com

FERNS & ALLIES *of the* NORTH WOODS

Printed in South Korea by Doosan
10 9 8 7 6 5 4 3 2 1   First Edition

Editorial Director: Mark Sparky Stensaas
Graphic Design: Kollath+Stensaas Publishing
Illustrations by Rick Kollath

ISBN-13: 978-1-936571-08-6

Table of Contents

Dedication	vi
Acknowledgements	vii
Welcome to the Magic	1
An Age of Ferns	8
No Birds or Bees Required	12
Searching for Ferns	16
How to Use this Field guide	20
Fiddleheads	22
Clubmosses	27
Common, One-cone Clubmosses	28
Bristly Clubmoss	30
Bog Clubmoss	32
Shining, Rock Firmosses	34
Northern, Mountain Firmosses	36
Prickly, Flat-branched, Hickey's Tree Clubmosses	38
Northern, Southern, Blue Ground Cedar	40
Spikemosses	42
Rock, Northern Spikemosses	44
Quillworts	43
Braun's, Lake Quillworts	46
Horsetails	48
Field, Meadow Horsetails	50
Water, Marsh Horsetails	52
Wood Horsetail	54
Tall, Smooth Scouring Rushes	56
Variegated Scouring Rush	58
Dwarf Scouring Rush	60
Moonworts	62
Northern Adder's Tongue	64
Common Moonwort	66
Least, Little Goblin Moonworts	68
Pale, Mingan, Spoon-leaf, Prairie Moonworts	70
Daisy-leaf, Triangle Moonworts	72
Leathery, Blunt-lobed, Rugulose Grapeferns	74
Dissected Grapefern	76
Rattlesnake Fern	78
Ferns of the Forest	
Eastern Bracken Fern	82
Northern Maidenhair Fern	84
Interrupted Fern	86
Northern Lady Fern	88
Silvery Spleenwort	90
New York, Hay-scented Ferns	92
Spinulose, Northern Wood Ferns	94
Male Fern	96
Evergreen Wood Fern	98
Marginal Wood Fern	100
Common, Limestone, Nahanni Oak Ferns	102
Northern, Broad Beech Ferns	104
Ferns of Wet Areas	
Ostrich Fern	106
Bead (Sensitive) Fern	108
Cinnamon Fern	110
Royal Fern	112
Goldie's Wood Fern	114
Crested Wood Fern	116
Northern Marsh Fern	118
Braun's, Northern Holly Ferns	120
Ferns of Rocky Areas	
Rock Polypody	122
Smooth, Purple Stem Cliff Brakes	124
Slender Cliff Brake	126
Walking, Hart's-Tongue Ferns	128
Maidenhair, Green Spleenworts	130
Fragrant Fern	132
Bulblet, Laurentian Bladder Ferns	134
Fragile Fern, Mackay's Brittle Fern	136
Smooth, Alpine Cliff Ferns	138
Rusty Cliff Fern	140
Oregon, Mountain Cliff Ferns	142
Glossary	144
Titles of Interest	150
Fern Groups	151
Photo Credits	151
Appendix	152
Index	160

Dedication

To all Wolf Ridge Naturalists,
pay attention, work hard and smile!

Acknowledgements

Everything we do has purpose. Reflecting on the completion of this field guide, I see now that my purpose has been less about the finished product and more about the process of learning about my community—both natural and social communities.

What I learned about my natural community—including ferns—is somewhat captured in this field guide as well as in *Lichens of the North Woods*. Nine years separate the publication of each field guide. As I learn more I have a desire to know more. My list of questions grows ever longer. I hope that never changes.

I learned even more about my social community. As with lichens, there has been a vital symbiosis at work here. Daily I recognize that what I gain from this symbiosis is more than what I provide. I hope that everyone in my community feels the same.

At this point I hope to acknowledge those of my community who continue to nourish my desire to notice the wonders surrounding us, to make meaningful connections to beautiful natural places, and to engage with the stories that are a part of the larger emerging story we all share. Though I could never properly capture every person, the examples that follow should capture the essence of what you all provide for me.

Lynden remains the model of a mentor I hope to be—perceptive, curious, empathetic and patient. MJ continues to demonstrate the qualities I encourage in learners—playful, reflective, creative and purposeful. Lori and Jenny never appear to run short of praise, hope, support and acceptance. Rick and Sparky impress me with their confidence, attention to detail, professionalism and determination.

Hundreds of others deserve to be listed here. I ask that you all recognize your personal qualities in the examples above and know that I value you all for what you contribute to our community. Thank you.

— Joe Walewski

Welcome to the Magic

Riffle through any naturalist's favorite field guide or notebook and you'll likely you'll find a pressed fern. Ferns are magical, beautiful, accessible and mysterious. I think we collect and keep them as one step toward capturing the magic for ourselves. I have done my best to press as much as possible of that magic within these pages.

For example, each spring I'm baffled by the immediate appearance and equally shocking disappearance of fertile Field Horsetail stems. Though they arise from the same root system that gives rise to the green branching stems we see all summer, those brown stems seem to *Presto* appear and then *Abracadabra* disappear. To me, it's equally mysterious and joyful as rabbits, coins or flowers in a magician's hands.

I set out to uncover the magic of *Equisetum arvense*. Dedicated, I watched the roadsides every day as the snow melted. Wouldn't you know it? They arose overnight! Hundreds of fertile, brown stems poked from the gravelly edges of the road and I missed them rising in the night.

I wouldn't miss the reverse. With a small cage encircling a healthy clump, I stopped by each and every day to photo- graph their progress. Soon, small green stems began to arise from the root system. My anticipation of the disappearance of those fertile brown stems grew.

I won't tell you what happened. Instead, I challenge you to do the same. Watch them come and go. Solve the mystery for yourself. In fact, throughout this field guide I hope to inspire you to engage in the magic and mystery of the ferns of our North Woods. To be sure, you will find answers in the pages that follow (names, descriptions, etc). You will also find dozens of questions and chal- lenges. That's part of the magic!

**The fertile
Field Horsetail,
*Equisetum arvense***

Pteridomania (aka "Fern Fever") spread throughout Europe during the mid and late 1800s and then travelled the world. Though not the British Invasion you might think of, its impact contin- ues to this day. You will find ferns growing in manicured gardens, under downspouts of homes and garages and even in terrariums. You'll see them as artistic flourishes on the covers of books, stationary and deep in the patterns of blacksmithed gates and fences. You'll certainly see them in images pertaining to both dinosaurs and fairies. Their magic sur- rounds us!

Cultures around the world have promoted myths and legends of ferns. Some believed that on June 23rd of each year you could capture the magic. According to legend, it was once thought that a captured fern "seed" would give the owner the power of invisibility. Stack twelve pewter plates under your favorite fern. At midnight, the invisible "seed" will fall from the fern and through the first 11 plates. You may then scoop that "seed" up and so capture the power of invisibility.

In Shakespeare's *Henry IV*, (Act 2 Scene 1) one of Falstaff's henchmen attempts to persuade a thief to join them and says, *"We steal as in a castle, cock-sure; we have the receipt of fern-seed, we walk invisible."* Because early botanists were unable to determine how ferns reproduced, it was thought that the seeds were invisible. According to the Doctrine of Signatures, characteristics of plants were visibly linked to their uses for humans. Leaf shaped like a liver? It might be useful for liver ailments. Almond shaped like an eye? It would be helpful with eyesight. Surely an invisible seed would confer invisibility to anyone who possessed it.

A manifestation of *Pteridomania*: the 19th century Wardian case.

Ferns, horsetails and clubmosses have other documented uses, though not many. In 1933, Ronald Good wrote the following in his *Plants and Human Economics*, *"The Pteridophytes (Ferns and their Allies) are also relatively useless."* Even if you discount the superhero power of invisibility, there remain a few interesting human uses. I'd say that pteridophytes are "somewhat useful."

More *Pteridomania*: an engraved, bucolic scene of Victorians admiring pteridophytes.

You might consider collecting the tender tasty fiddleheads of the Ostrich Fern in early spring. Steamed or lightly boiled, the fiddleheads serve as a tasty vegetable similar to asparagus. A touch of browned butter and a dash of salt make them very tasty indeed. Though you will find literature citing other ferns used for food, the only species that is both tasty and non-carcinogenic in our area is *Matteuccia struthiopteris*, the Ostrich Fern.

Equisetum (horsetails and scouring rushes) continues to be used for sanding and polishing fine wood. Silica in the plant provides grit for a very fine "sand paper." That grit remains in the plant fibers and does not fill in the pores of the wood. Fittingly, classy violin-makers still collect and use *Equisetum* for the final work on their "fiddle heads."

Bracken has been used for a variety of dyes. An olive green dye can be achieved from leaves boiled for 20 minutes with mordant of alum and copper. Dark yellow dyes can be made by simmering the rhizome in water for 2 hours. Bring the wool and water to a boil with alum for another 2 hours. Forest Horsetail has been used in Scandinavia to produce a grayish yellow dye.

Though ferns have been used as a source of fiber in many parts of the world, little has been done with the species we find in the North Woods. The black stems of Maidenhair Fern have been worked into the designs of basket making. So too have the boiled brown roots of Bracken Fern. In some places, clubmosses have been collected for wreath

Utilitarian ferns: delicious Ostrich Fern fiddleheads, and nature's fine grit *Equisetum* at work smoothing a man-made violin "fiddle head."

making, but be careful not to over-collect and harm the population if you choose to do this.

Have a blast with clubmoss spores. Available as Dragon's Breath, you can purchase a jar of spores for use in magic shows—you have surely seen this before. If you find a healthy population of clubmosses in the Fall, collect a few of the strobili. Dry the strobili in a paper bag for a week or so and gently pour the yellow powder into a jar for long-term storage. Mix spores and air with a flame for a shockingly memorable flash!

If ferns are not already growing very near you, careful transplants of the more common forest ferns might be interesting. Never collect without permission and never collect species of concern or species that are not obviously thriving. During the 19th century, Wardian Cases were all the rage. Invented in 1829 by Dr. Nathaniel Ward, the large glass cases served as tiny greenhouses suitable for ferns. As an early version of terrariums, a Wardian Case serves as a classy way to grow and display ferns and mosses in your home.

The flames produced by *Lycopodium lagopus* spores are a bit orange. What will you get with spores from other species?

Perhaps you are more like me and simply want to search for them. That is precisely where this book comes in handy. Between these pages you'll find dozens of species to learn– more than just a simple name. Put this in your pocket or backpack and enjoy searching for ferns as you hike forests or paddle lakes of the North Woods. Welcome to the magic!

What is Included in this Book

Often referred to as ferns and fern allies or pteridophytes (literally, "winged plants"), this field guide covers the entire collection of non-flowering vascular plants in the North Woods. Consider that: major examples of ALL of the non-flowering vascular plants of our area are collected here in one handy source. Of course a book covering this topic in Central America would necessarily be much, much larger.

Collectively, pteridophytes comprise about 3 percent of the vascular plant species of North America. We can find nearly 100 species in the North Woods. North America is home to nearly 450 species. Europe has about 175 species. All of China has an estimated 2,000 species. Tiny Costa Rica boasts of nearly 1,000 species! Worldwide there are about 12,000 species.

Ferns, horsetails, clubmosses, quillworts and spikemosses comprise the entire assemblage of non-flowering vascular plants found in the North Woods today. Some are quite common and others extremely rare. Because some freely interbreed and form hybrids, it's hard to absolutely identify some of the organisms you may come across. We'll leave those mysteries for professional botanists to solve. Though a few other species of quillwort, for example, can be found in our range, only the most commonly encountered species are included in this book. Besides, you would have to look closely at spore structures to identify them anyway.

Ferns vary, of course, but the general structure is feather-like in appearance. The main stem is composed of a stipe at the base with a rachis above and the branching leaflets are variously divided from speies to species. I once listened to a call-in radio garden show in which a man asked about caring for some ferns in his yard. When the host asked for the kind of ferns, the caller replied, "oh, the kind you'd find in a forest." When observed closely, it is obvious that they are not all the same. For example, though most of our "typical" ferns have spore-bearing structures on the backs of their broad and finely dissected leaves, not all follow that pattern.

Osmundopsida are the most primitive living family and are often referred to as "flowering ferns" because of their unique spore structures and arrangements. They first appeared during the Permian Period (from 280-230 million years ago). A lot happened during the Permian Period—Pangea formed, gymnosperms evolved and reptiles diversified. The era ended with Earth's largest mass extinction in which 90 percent of all marine forms and 70 percent of all landforms died out.

Though scientists are still attempting to find solid evidence to explain why the extinction occurred, all of the theories relate to an increased global temperature of 5 degrees Celsius. It may have been caused by basalt eruptions releasing carbon dioxide, hydrogen sulfide gas released from deep ocean reservoirs or methane released from slowly rising ocean temperatures. Global climate change led to extinctions and a shift from the Permian Period to the Triassic Period.

Though most of the species that ever existed in Osmundopsida have gone extinct, just a few more than 20 species remain worldwide. Among them is our oldest living fern species dating back to 180 million years ago, *Osmunda cinnamomea*, the Cinnamon Fern. It remains one of the few species still existing today that also existed among dinosaurs roaming the earth from 230-65 million years ago (Triassic, Jurassic and Cretaceous Periods).

More than 80 percent of the world's ferns are True Ferns. Most arose and diversified about 100 million years ago. In addition to *Osmunda*, ferns such as Bracken, Lady Fern, Rock Polypody, Oak Fern and Spleenwort are among the True Ferns. Also called *leptosporangiate ferns*, they produce spores in sporangium each containing up to 512, as few as 16 or most commonly 32 spores.

Some of our most magical of ferns, the moonworts, are known as *eusporangiate ferns*. Others include the grapeferns, horsetails and scouring rushes. The spore-bearing structures are unique from group to group, yet they all produce vast amounts of spores—thousands per sporangium.

Ferns and Equisetum are the most closely related among the five groups of non-flowering vascular plants. Horsetails and scouring rushes (*Equisetum*) are distinctly ancient-looking. Many have an upright stem with branches originating along that stem and a spore-bearing "cone" at the top. Related to Calamites that were abundant in the Late

Carboniferous swamps, there are 15 species worldwide belonging to a single genus *Equisetum*. The North Woods is home to 9 of those species.

Clubmosses, quillworts and spikemosses are all associated more specifically as **lycophytes**. Some clubmosses share the common names of "princess pine" or "ground pine." Since they are neither mosses nor pines, these names are misleading. Spikemosses are easily overlooked members of the rock outcrop community. Small and similar in appearance to true mosses, spikemosses can be a challenge to locate. Quillworts require wading or even snorkeling to observe. They have leaves similar in shape to porcupine quills and are found in shallow shorelines or even in as deep as 10 feet of clear, cold water.

The first step in the process of identification requires that you identify your plant within one of the main groups: clubmoss, spikemoss, quillwort, horsetail or fern. In this guide, the ferns are further subdivided to make identification a bit easier. *Eusporangiate ferns* form one section including *Botrychium* and adder's tongue. *Leptosporangiate ferns* are further subdivided based on habitat including *Ferns of Forests, Ferns of Wet Areas* and *Ferns of Rocky Areas*. Though this clearly bears no connection to formal taxonomy, it can be useful in the field for ease of identification. When looking at a community of ferns, be sure to look at several specimens in order to better see species variation throughout as well as the most common botanical structures (for example, separate fertile stalks, distinct branching, hairs or lack of hairs, colors, sizes, etc).

Clubmosses (page 27)

A small-leaved plant variously resembling moss or seedlings of spruce, fir, pine or cedar; in most species, the spores are borne in a special structure called a strobili; some species have their spores borne in special structures among the small leaves and attached to the main stem.

Clubmoss

Spikemosses (page 42)

This can look like a moss or even a very small clubmoss; its distinct spores are visible among the leaf axils as megaspores and microspores.

Spikemoss

Quillworts (page 43)

A distinct aquatic plant with awl or quill-like leaves originating from the center of a circular clump at varying depths in cool, clear water.

Quillwort

Horsetails (page 48)

One main central stalk divided into smaller sections with nodes in between; often with branches, but some species are distinctly non-branched; fertile stages include a "cone" which releases spores.

Horsetail

Eusporangiate ferns (page 63)

These plants are divided into two main botanical structures—the leaf is called a tropophore and the stem bearing small clusters of grape-like, bead-like sporangia is the sporophore; this group of ferns can be further divided into grapeferns (with the sporophore and tropophore arising as separate stalks), moonworts (with the sporophore and tropophore attached above ground on a common main stem) and adder's tongue (similar to moonworts but tropophore is one oval simple leaf).

Moonwort

Leptosporangiate ferns (page 80)

These remaining ferns look like a "typical fern" with a variously cut main leaf that most commonly has spore bearing structures in small clusters on the back of that main leaf frond; the fronds are either once-cut into distinct pinnae or further divided into smaller pinnules and maybe even pinnulets; some of the species bear spores on unique structures that may be connected to the frond or may grow on separated stalks.

Oak Fern

A 19th century engraved landscape imaging the Carboniferous Period.

An Age of Ferns

The Carboniferous Period

Much of our electricity—over 75 percent today—is produced in power plants dependent upon ferns. Okay, not ferns directly, but the remains of those ferns in the form of coal serve as a major source of our electricity. Over time, plant parts and spores collected in massive layers on the edges of inland seas. Sediments covered them. With time, heat and pressure, the plant layers underwent chemical and physical changes. Rich carbon deposits remained as coal.

During the Carboniferous Period, Calamites (ancient precursors of today's *Equisetum*) towered up to 100 feet tall, grew a bark-like substance and produced vast quantities of spores. Cannel coal is fossilized calamites and *Lycopodium* spores. Some cannel coal seams have been found as thick as 1.5 feet. This would have required 12 feet of spores to produce. The amount of spores floating through the Carboniferous skies staggers the imagination.

White Rot fungus (a member of *Agaricomycetes*) is responsible for decay of lignin, the complex polymer found in tree bark. This fungus did not exist for the first 60 million years of pteridophytes. The rise of White Rot fungus aligns with the end of the Carboniferous Period and it had a major impact on the ensuing ecology.

We no longer live in an age of major coal formation. We live in an age of human-influence with major fossil fuel burning. Coal and oil have contributed significantly to the changes we are witnessing today. Change happens—true. Major changes are associated with each boundary of geologic, deep time (the shift from Permian to Triassic, for example). Current human change may be no less natural than other major extinctions. The difference is that we have made conscious, moral choices causing this sixth major extinction. Because of the massive influence we humans are having on the planet, some scientists have suggested that we are at a transition and the Anthropocene (*anthropo* meaning human) should be added as the next epoch in the Quaternary Period (Pleistocene, Holocene, then Anthropocene). In her new book, *Great Tide Rising*, Kathleen Dean Moore offers up a better suggestion focused on the evidence left behind in the rock layers rather than the source. She suggests that Unforgiveable-crimescene or Obscene are more appropriate. Hard to disagree with that.

Peering back in time, at least as far as the late Devonian Period of 360 million years ago (mya), fossil evidence suggests that ferns and related non-flowering vascular plants were a dominant feature of the landscape. This was a time period when continental landmasses clumped together as Laurasia and Gondwanaland along the equator; temperatures and carbon dioxide levels were much higher; insects were giants and some dragonflies had 6 foot wingspans; much of the fungus and other decomposers common today were not yet a significant part of the ecology; dinosaurs were not present yet; and the plant world looked quite different without flowering plants. Spore-producing plants ruled the landscape. In fact, major precursors of our current fern assemblage were represented by impres-

Basically unchanged for 210,000,000 years, relatives of this Cinnamon Fern tickled the bellies of all the greatest dinosaurs. But dinosaurs went extinct, and yet Cinnamon Fern continues strong.

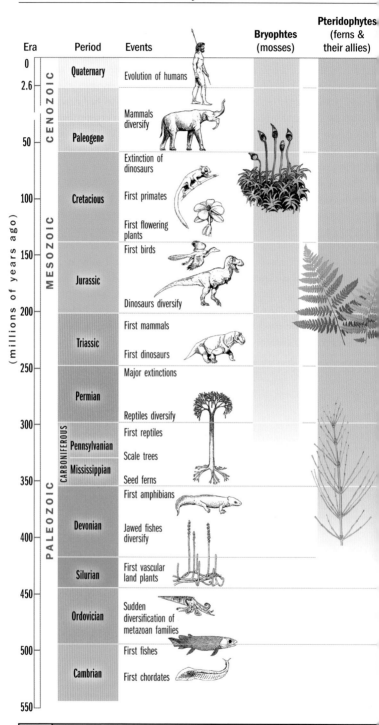

Era	Period	Events	Bryophtes (mosses)	Pteridophytes (ferns & their allies)
CENOZOIC	Quaternary	Evolution of humans		
	Paleogene	Mammals diversify		
MESOZOIC	Cretaceous	Extinction of dinosaurs / First primates / First flowering plants		
	Jurassic	First birds / Dinosaurs diversify		
	Triassic	First mammals / First dinosaurs		
PALEOZOIC	Permian	Major extinctions / Reptiles diversify		
	Pennsylvanian	First reptiles / Scale trees		
	Mississippian	Seed ferns		
	Devonian	First amphibians / Jawed fishes diversify		
	Silurian	First vascular land plants		
	Ordovician	Sudden diversification of metazoan families		
	Cambrian	First fishes / First chordates		

(millions of years ago)

0
2.6
50
100
150
200
250
300
350
400
450
500
550

CARBONIFEROUS

Gymnosperms (conifers)	Angiosperms (flowering plants)

sive 100-foot high horsetail-like and clubmoss-like plants.

Today's ferns are not the same species that were present during the Carboniferous, yet, some species, including the Cinnamon Fern, Royal Fern and Interrupted Fern, remain from the Cretaceous Period (180 mya) when dinosaurs roamed the land. During the extinction of dinosaurs, many ferns also suffered extinction. What remain today are species capable of growing in low-light conditions. A unique chemical receptor (*neochrome*) evolved that gave these new species an ability to grow in the shade of dominant conifers and flowering plants.

About 180 mya a virus picked up the neochrome gene in a hornwort (related to mosses) and transferred it via horizontal gene transfer to a fern. This is one of many naturally formed genetically modified organisms (GMOs) that have contributed to evolution. Neochrome provides the ability to photosynthesize in the extreme red and blue wavelengths of light. In essence, many ferns of today are capable of photosynthesizing under a much wider light spectrum and can take advantage of marginal growing situations.

Many of the current families of ferns appeared roughly 145 million years ago. The species we see today are certainly much smaller than those of the Carboniferous. Structurally, however, they look much the same. Wandering among the ferns in our forests today is very much like wandering among a Carboniferous forest in miniature.

No Birds or Bees Required

Reproduction in Ferns, Clubmosses, Horsetails

All pteridophytes reproduce by *spores*. Until the mystery was solved in the sixteenth century, people did not understand how ferns reproduced and assumed they grew from invisible seeds. Whereas seeds are complex, multicellular structures containing all a plant needs in order to grow, spores are usually *haploid* (they have half the chromosomes of a parent plant) and unicellular. Don't let this fool you, though, as spores serve the parent plant well. Pteridophytes, mosses and many other organisms that reproduce by spores are able to spread and thrive in many habitats.

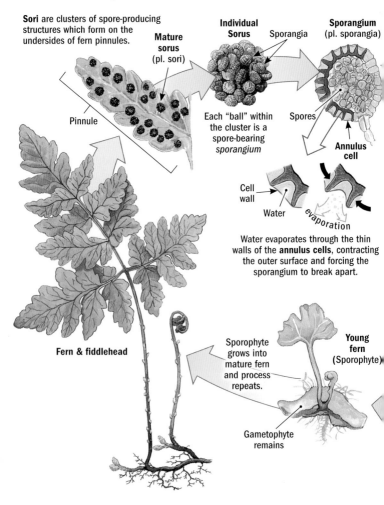

Sori are clusters of spore-producing structures which form on the undersides of fern pinnules.

Mature sorus (pl. sori)

Pinnule

Individual Sorus   Sporangia

Each "ball" within the cluster is a spore-bearing *sporangium*

Sporangium (pl. sporangia)

Spores

Annulus cell

Cell wall

Water

evaporation

Water evaporates through the thin walls of the **annulus cells**, contracting the outer surface and forcing the sporangium to break apart.

Fern & fiddlehead

Sporophyte grows into mature fern and process repeats.

Young fern (Sporophyte)

Gametophyte remains

Ferns and other pteridophytes usually undergo an alternation of generations. As spores successfully germinate, they develop into a small, green, heart-shaped *gametophyte* (sometimes called a *prothallus*). Gametophytes serve as structures for sexual reproduction. The male *antheridia* and female *archegonia* are both present on a single gametophyte. As such, self-fertilization is possible. In nature, gametophytes tend to pass through all-archegonial and then all-antheridial phases. This promotes cross-fertilization. In addition, the female archegonia produce substances that promote the development of male structures in nearby gametophytes.

Just as you would expect, sperm swim from the antheridia to the archegonia. Another substance is produced to attract sperm to the egg in the archegonia. After successful fertilization, the egg divides and develops toward the second phase of reproduction as a *sporophyte*. All

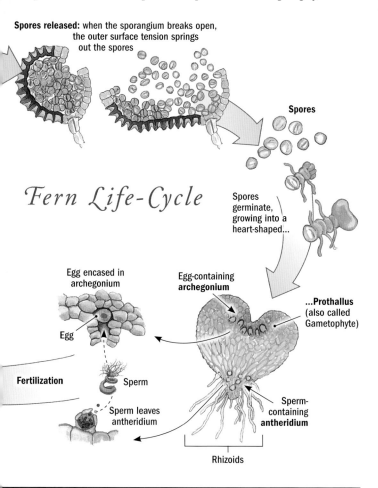

Spores released: when the sporangium breaks open, the outer surface tension springs out the spores

Spores

Fern Life-Cycle

Spores germinate, growing into a heart-shaped...

...**Prothallus** (also called Gametophyte)

Egg encased in archegonium

Egg-containing **archegonium**

Egg

Fertilization

Sperm

Sperm leaves antheridium

Sperm-containing **antheridium**

Rhizoids

of the structures referred to in this book for identification are part of this second phase of the alternating generations. All species portraits are of the sporophyte stage.

You might search for germinated spores in moist exposed areas, on rotting logs and mixed in with mosses. In some cases, you may find the resulting gametophytes in groups of a thousand or more. The gametophytes are often greenish, flat and have projecting hairs that may serve as an anchor or for water uptake. Gametophytes underground are yellow to brown, a bit fleshy and oblong and are extremely hard to find.

In contrast, the sporophytes are large and quite visible…if you notice them, of course. Sporophytes produce the spores that started the entire process. These spores are located in *sporangia* which are generally located on leaves or modified leaves. In some cases (as in the Ostrich Fern), a species will form two different structures—one is *sterile* while the other is *fertile*. In the *Botrychium*, the fertile portion is called a sporophore and the sterile portion is called a tropophore.

Though each species produces a different number of spores, the quantity of spores floating in our atmosphere is astounding. It has been estimated that a single Bead (Sensitive) Fern would produce upwards of 450,000 spores. A single Marginal Wood Fern frond can produce about 52,000,000 spores.

Worldwide, pteridophyte spores may be white, yellow, orange, green, brown or black. They are often between 20-60 micrometers in diameter and almost invisible without a microscope. For comparison, human hair averages about 100 micrometers in diameter. In spikemosses and quillworts, spores come in two sizes and serve specific purposes in reproduction. Male spores are smaller (20-30 micrometers). Female spores can range from 200-700 micrometers and are readily observed with a decent hand lens. Spore shape and structure can be used to help identification sometimes to the species level.

Spores can be distributed over long distances by wind dispersal. In general, pteridophytes tend to have much larger ranges than flowering plants. Spores germinate quite readily under suitable conditions and can sometimes remain viable for more than a decade. Green spores (those containing chlorophyll) must germinate in a matter of days before they die. *Botrychium* spores must associate with a fungal host in complete darkness deep in the soil for germination.

Only a tiny fraction of spores successfully germinate. In fact, pteridophytes reproduce under a variety of strategies beyond the classic alternation of generations. These include many methods of vegetative reproduction, hybridization of all sorts and even growing from a gametophyte into a sporophyte without fertilization. Gasp! Some pteridophytes simply won't follow the rules.

Vegetative reproduction occurs most frequently. Bracken Ferns develop massive networks of *rhizomes* that branch out and produce extensive colonies that may cover 1-2 acres and be upwards of 1000 years old. Prairie Moonwort produces tiny *gemmae* on the stem and roots. These gemmae break off in the soil and grow into new plants. Some *Huperzia* do the same. Bulblet Bladder Ferns form special bulblets (like tiny peas) on the rachis. They fall from the parent plant and can form large colonies on steep slopes—almost like a waterfall of ferns. These are only a few examples.

Fir clubmoss gemmae ready to go forth and populate the Earth.

A bulbet on the eponymously named Bulbet Bladder Fern.

Hybridization—the reproduction between two related, but different species –occurs among the ferns quite readily in some situations. It's easy to imagine spores of different species germinating next to each other. This occurs in *Equisetum* and *Diphasiastrum*, for example. The hybrid plants retain characteristics of both parents. The spores of these hybrids are almost always infertile. Under a microscope, it's possible to see malformed spores to confirm that it is a hybrid. In some cases, species that hybridize may have normal spore formation resulting in fertile spores and a possible new species. As if this wasn't already mind-blowing enough, hybrids may be *diploid* (the normal 2 sets of chromosomes), *triploid* (3 sets of chromosomes) or even *tetraploid* (4 sets of chromosomes).

Leptosporangiate ferns, especially those in dry, rocky areas, benefit from another reproductive strategy. Under *apogamy* the spore germinates into a gametophyte that then directly grows into a sporophyte without fertilization. This eliminates the need for moisture and the transfer of sperm to egg. Narrow Beech Fern and Smooth Cliff Brake are examples of ferns that benefit from apogamy.

Some of our species are associated with *mycorrhizal fungi*, especially the moonworts, grapeferns and some clubmosses. Pale brown or yellow gametophytes germinate below ground and associate with a fungus. Both partners in this association receive some benefit. The pteridophyte receives nutrients from its fungal partner while developing and reproducing by the classic alternation of generations.

Finally, spikemosses and quillworts vary from the norm in that they produce male and female spores. Male spores (*microspores*) are tiny and produced in large quantities. Female spores (*megaspores*) are visible to the naked eye and far fewer per plant. You will need to look closely with a hand lens at the megaspores to positively identify quillworts to species.

Reproduction can be quite varied and magical among the pterido-phytes. Though some of that magic has been discovered, there is still much to learn. Field naturalists and lab scientists continue to uncover the magic.

Searching For Ferns

Where?

Though precursors of today's pteridophytes thrived in swampy conditions, we now find them in the North Woods in very diverse habitats including wet areas, rocky outcrops, disturbed areas and forests of all types. Worldwide they are more abundant in tropical rainforests, yet they can be found on all continents and islands except for sterile polar regions and extreme deserts. They can even be found growing beyond the Arctic Circle.

Wet areas: Cinnamon Fern, Bead (Sensitive) Fern, Northern Marsh Fern, Crested Wood Fern, Water Horsetail, Bog Clubmoss and Quillworts are often distinct components of wetlands. Expect to find exceptions to the rules. I have found Royal Fern thriving in both knee-deep water and in a seemingly dry forest. Some of these species take advantage of liquid water early in spring—you will see them among the first to begin their new growth. I have also seen the Crested Wood Fern fiddleheads begin to unfurl in late June. I only assume that the mossy substrate below harbored ice into summer. Marsh Fern is often abundant in open grassy areas and on edges of lakes. Bog Clubmoss and Cinnamon Fern serve as indicator species of wetlands.

Rocky Outcrops: Rock Spikemoss, Fragrant Wood Fern, Fragile Bladder Fern, cliff ferns, firmosses and cliff brakes are well adapted to colonize this marginal habitat. Growing among mosses, lichens, tena-cious cedar trees and other scrappy flowering and non-flowering plants, they obviously aren't the only vegetation able to survive the harsh con-ditions. Ferns of rocky areas (cliffs, boulders, talus) tend to be able to withstand drying. They are often small, tufted and somewhat leathery. Be sure to be very careful when looking for ferns here—watch your step for safety and also take time to slow down and look very closely. Some of our most rare species may exist in hidden crevices nearby.

Edgar Wherry (1885-1982), author of *A Fern Guide*, was particularly nterested in rocky habitats. He noticed that acidic rocks (granite, quartz-te and sandstone) have a particular set of species including *Huperzia* ind *Asplenium*. Similarly, calcareous rocks (shales and limestones, for example) provide homes for particular *Aspleniums* and *Pellaeas*.

Disturbed Areas: Hardy plants quick to grow in any condition find success in pathways, along roadsides and in association with areas recent-y altered and opened by windthrown trees, landslides, fires and Beaver activity. Disturbed and second-growth areas may be home to Bracken and Field Horsetail—both can even become "weedy." In seemingly simi-ar conditions you might also begin to find varied clubmosses and moon-worts. In fact, disturbed areas can provide some of the most magical of rewards to those who are curious and perseverant. Don't pass them up.

Forests: Prime habitat for most of our pteridophytes is the mesic for-est. Look for *Huperzia, Lycopodium, Equisetum, Osmunda, Dryopteris, Polystichum, Thelypteris* and *Athyrium*. Take time to explore stands of well established maple, pine or oak, for example. Mixed, younger forests can be diverse, but some plant and animal species fill niches only found deep in those ancient, continuous forests. The Little Goblin Moonwort, for example, is very much at risk of disappearance due to both logging and invading exotic earthworms. Some of the most magical places you might encounter are those cathedral-like forests—towering trunks with no middle understory, rather a wide open expanse of varying shorter plants including some patches maybe of Northern Maidenhair Fern, Ostrich Fern and perhaps interspersed clumps of Evergreen Wood Fern.

When?

You can look for ferns in all seasons. This guide aims to help you interpret the scene and identify the species regardless of season or stage. In particular, you will notice the section devoted specifically to "fiddleheads." Turn there if you find a fiddlehead and then follow the reference to the species description where you will find the full-grown specimen and maybe even images from fall and winter.

Spring: As the snowpack melts, look for fern fronds that were flat-tened to the ground by the first snows. Evergreen Wood Fern will remain green all winter. It is not actually evergreen and might be better described as "winter green" since it holds onto the green all winter. As the soils continue to warm, brown fertile stems of the Field Horsetail will emerge and then disappear a week or so later.

Spring is most noted by emerging fiddleheads. A fiddlehead is sim-ply the emerging growth of leptosporangiate ferns. Look for Interrupted Ferns and Lady Ferns. You will also have a narrow window of opportunity to collect some tender Ostrich Fern fiddleheads for a meal or two. More on this topic is covered in the *Fiddlehead* section.

Summer: Far and away the most common time to look for ferns, there is much to discover in summer. Some ferns, like Bracken Fern and Crested Wood Fern, will continue to send up fiddleheads as summer progresses. A majority of the ferns will have already formed completely. Most of the photos in this guide represent growth in this season.

Some *Botrychium* species may arise one summer and remain dormant for many summers to follow. Don't be surprised to return to a location and be unable to find the mysterious moonworts in the same place you found them last summer.

Depending upon the moisture and other conditions, cliff ferns may thrive or appear to just barely hang in there at various times during a single summer. The Rusty Cliff Fern can appear almost dead and then revive to a brighter green after a dousing rainfall.

Fall: As the end of the growing season nears, some ferns succumb to early frosts. Sensitive (Bead) Fern is not really all that sensitive, but it does brown after a hard frost. Bracken Ferns will begin to speckle too. Pay attention to the Cinnamon Fern—the fronds can become so brilliantly orange-brown you might feel the need to wear sunglasses to look at it.

In early Fall, you can expect to find ripening strobili atop clubmosses. Occasionally you might even notice spores puffing into the air while walking through a particularly mature patch. It is a sure sign that fall is about to come to a close when you notice the seemingly "bleached bones" of the Field Horsetail.

Some Wood Ferns will turn brown and fall back to the ground. The Evergreen Wood Fern undergoes an interesting change; in preparation for winter, the base of its stipe (nearest the ground) will soften and allow the entire frond to lay flat to the ground. A good covering of snow protects the frond from the harsh drying winds of winter. Snowpack changes due to climate change will certainly result in some range changes for these species.

Every season provides for new adventures and discoveries. You will certainly find some habitats easier to explore in winter; spring provides for the magic of new growth; the green of summer is lush and vibrant; and any hike through a colorful fall forest will be enhanced by the awareness of pteridophytes all around.

Winter: Though winter may seem to be the wrong time of year to search for pteridophytes, don't be mistaken. The fertile stems of Bead (Sensitive) Fern and Ostrich Fern remain standing tall above the snow line. Expect to see them while skiing or snowshoeing. Curled fronds of the Fragrant Fern hang tight in rock crevices. While exploring among arger moss covered boulders, the surprisingly bright green fronds of Rock Polypody will certainly brighten your day. Henry David Thoreau noticed and wrote of their "fresh and cheerful communities."

Spring

Summer

Fall

Winter

How to use this Field Guide

Order

The species included in this field guide—collectively referred to as pteridophytes—are first arranged by groups: clubmosses, spikemosses, quillworts, horsetails, moonworts and ferns. Ferns are further subdivided by typical habitat (forests, wet areas and rocky areas). If you cannot locate a likely species in the habitat section, check other sections. Ferns have been known to ignore the rules. In spring, turn to the *Fiddleheads* section to identify unfurling fronds.

Pteridophyte Names

As with all organisms, pteridophytes have both common names and scientific names. Common names will certainly vary depending on regional traditions. You will also find that some of the scientific names may differ among varying field guides. Scientific names routinely change over time as we learn more about the organisms. For this guide we have chosen to use most of the recent names found in *Flora of North America, Volume 2: Pteridophytes and Gymnosperms,* published in 1993. Consult the Appendix to learn more.

Photos

All organisms can vary dramatically depending upon genetics and local growing conditions. We chose to include a variety of photos that might cover the variability even through the seasons. We also try to show a wider shot of the pteridophyte in its habitat. Close up images showing diagnostic traits for that species are also included.

Habitat

Beneath each photo on the left hand page is a more specific list of habitats where you might find that species.

Description

Description includes the best distinguishing characteristics with as little technical jargon as possible. It is important that users familiarize themselves with the names of the parts of the ferns, clubmosses and horsetails as these terms are used. Part names are in bold type.

Nature Notes

Nature Notes are fascinating bits of natural history, unique uses or detailed descriptions of structures that provide a more complete understanding of that species. Population trends, ecology, naming history and other historical accounts are also included.

Similar Species

Here you will find information regarding species that are very similar and easily confused with the main species. Sometimes these are rare spe-

ies in our area (scientific name shown) and sometimes species included
n the book (page number shown). Look closely at the maps to deter-
nine the possibility of each species in your specific location.

Glossary

Check out the glossary for easy to understand meanings for some tricky
erms found in this or other field guides.

Habitats where this fern typically occurs.

The main photo is a diagnostic image of that species.

Photos showing plant details can be found on the right-hand page.

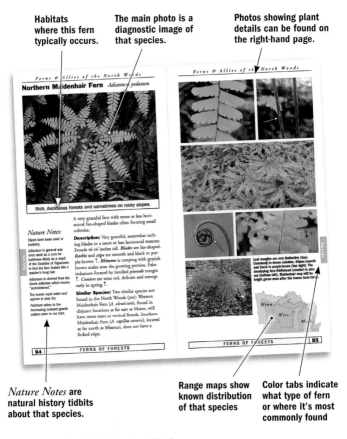

Nature Notes are natural history tidbits about that species.

Range maps show known distribution of that species

Color tabs indicate what type of fern or where it's most commonly found

Quick Color Tabs make identification easy

clubmoss	spikemoss	quillwort	horsetail	moonwort

Tabs for types of pteridophytes help get you quickly to the right section of the guide.

forests	wet areas	rocky areas

These tabs delineate what type of habitat/substrate the typical ferns grow in.

Fiddleheads

Curled to protect the tender tip while emerging from the soil, a fiddlehead looks much like the scrollwork on the handle of a violin. The tight curl is termed *circinate vernation*. Fiddleheads are also sometimes called *croziers* after the curled head of a shephard's or Bishop's staff.

You may be tempted to eat fiddleheads, but beware. Not all fiddleheads are edible as some sources imply. The only fern edible in our area is the Ostrich Fern. Bracken Fern contains a known carcinogen (ptaquiloside or PTA) and some of the other fiddleheads (like Lady Fern and Cinnamon Fern) lack the palatability to warrant the time collecting and preparing—not to mention the impact on the growth of the local population. *Other fiddleheads worldwide are edible, but only the Ostrich Fern is worth the effort in the North Woods.*

The primary purpose of this section, therefore, is for identification purposes instead of collecting and preparation. Some fiddleheads have distinct hairs or scales. They will often wither as the fern continues to grow. Evidence of these structures sometimes remains if you look hard enough. Other fiddleheads may be brightly colored. As you begin to notice fiddleheads emerging, turn to this section and page through the images to see if you can find a match. More importantly, note the location of what you are seeing and return later in the season to confirm your identification. Write your notes in the margins of this section and keep developing your knowledge of ferns in every season including early spring.

Eastern Bracken Fern (page 82)

Northern Maidenhair (page 84)

Fiddleheads

Interrupted Fern (page 86)

Northern Lady Fern (page 88)

Silvery Spleenwort (page 90)

New York Fern (page 92)

Spinulose Wood Fern (page 94)

Male Fern (page 96)

Fiddleheads

Evergreen Wood Fern (page 98)

Common Oak Fern (page 102)

Broad Beech Fern (page 104)

Northern Beech Fern (page 104)

Ostrich Fern (page 106)

Bead (Sensitive) Fern (page 108)

Fiddleheads

Cinnamon Fern (page 110)

Royal Fern (page 112)

Goldie's Wood Fern (page 114)

Crested Wood Fern (page 116)

Northern Marsh Fern (page 118)

Braun's Holly Fern (page 120)

Fiddleheads

Holly Fern (page 120)

Rock Polypody (page 122)

Fragrant Fern (page 132)

Bulbet Bladder Fern (page 134)

Fragile Fern (page 136)

Rusty Cliff Fern (page 140)

Clubmosses

When identifying clubmosses, note the presence of growing yellowish-green strobili or even light brown strobili persisting from the previous year. Look also for branching above the ground and the presence or absence of an above-ground runner.

Though it is unlikely that you will mistake a clubmoss for a spikemoss, or vice versa, note the size. Spikemosses are significantly smaller.

At first glance, it will appear that *Huperzia* lack spore structures. Bend the main stem back near the upper portion and you will readily notice the spore structures growing in obvious bands. If you find *Huperzia*, also note the presence of gemmae either at the top or scattered throughout.

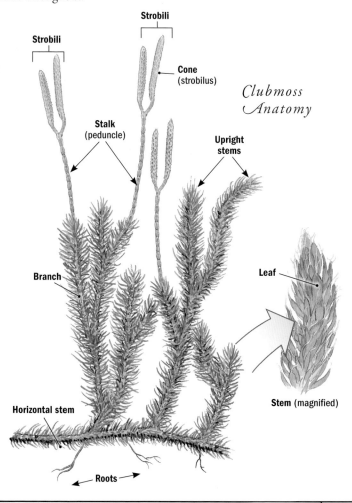

Strobili

Strobili

Cone
(strobilus)

*Clubmoss
Anatomy*

Stalk
(peduncle)

Upright
stems

Branch

Leaf

Horizontal stem

Stem (magnified)

Roots

Common Clubmoss *Lycopodium clavatum*

Sandy soils of mixed forests, fields and edges.

Nature Notes:

Also called Running Pine or Wolf's Claw Clubmoss, Linnaeus named this entire group *Lycopodium* because of what he saw in this species. *Lycos* means "wolf" and *pod* means "foot." He saw a wolf foot. Look for yourself.

As with all lycopods, the spores can be collected and used as flash powder. Never over-collect any local population. Consider the 1-in-10 rule; collect no more than one for every ten you see. Simply place the collected strobili in a dry place undisturbed for a week or so. When you pull out the dried strobili, tap them to knock loose the remaining spores. You can then experiment with varying flames to see the results. Enjoy!

Obviously creeping clubmoss with upright branching stems.

Description: Creeping plant with upright branched yellowish-green stems. Horizontal stems near the surface often form dense colonies. Upright stems are 4-10 inches tall and densely leafy, branching 3-6 times ↑ at various lengths. *Leaves* are about third inch long and narrow with a hair-like tip. If *strobili* are present, you will most often find two ↑ distinct 3 inch long "cones" at the end of a single 1.5-3 inch long stalk.

Similar Species: One-cone Clubmoss (*Lycopodium lagopus*) are found in open, grassy fields and open woodlands. Look for upright stems branching only once or twice ↑. Also, search for single strobili ↑ at the end of a single long stalk. If two are present on a single stalk, they should be attached at the same point rather than obviously separated.

clubmoss

Stem magnified

One-cone Clubmoss
Lycopodium lagopus

One-cone Clubmoss
Lycopodium lagopus

Horizontal stems creep across the surface. Strobili usually bear at least 2 distinct "cones." One-cone Clubmoss, not surprisingly, has strobili with only 1 "cone" (bottom right).

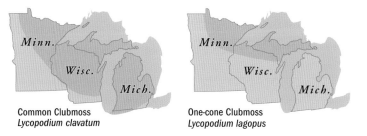

Minn.

Wisc.

Mich.

Common Clubmoss
Lycopodium clavatum

Minn.

Wisc.

Mich.

One-cone Clubmoss
Lycopodium lagopus

Bristly Clubmoss *Spinulum annotinum*

In moist mixed forests and rocky places among conifers.

Stiff, bottlebrush-like clubmoss.

Nature Notes:

Formerly known as *Lycopodium annotinum*.

Annotinus means "belonging to the year" which refers to the annual constrictions that are very obvious along the entire stem.

How long do these clubmosses grow? Count the annual constrictions on this species for yourself and compare to other individuals in this population or in other forests. What do you notice in general?

Description: Stiff, prickly bottlebrush ↑ appearance with a single strobili at the tip. Dark evergreen leaves are about 0.3 inches long with toothed edges and a very sharp tip. Horizontal stem very near the surface. Upright round stems about 6 inches tall branching at the base. *Strobilus* 1.5 inches long, sessile ↑ and usually only one per branch.

Similar Species: Compared to Firmoss (*Huperzia* sp.), Bristly Clubmoss are much more organized and spreading. Common Clubmoss (pg. 28) have long-stalked strobili while Bristly Clubmoss have strobili attached immediately at the tip of the bristly stem.

Stiff, orderly, sharp-tipped leaves grace the stem giving this species a bristly appearance. Single "cone" is sessile to the stem.

Minn.

Wisc.

Mich.

Bog Clubmoss   *Lycopodiella inundata*

clubmoss

Limited to bogs, fens and marshes among mosses or sandy soils.

A very small, creeping plant with a bushy-tailed upright stem.

Nature Notes:

Inundata means covered by water. Formerly known as *Lycopodium inundata*.

This lycopod grows among the mosses and even looks much like a moss. So what's the difference between club-moss and moss? All of the organisms in this field guide are vascular plants. Mosses lack a vascular system. Vascular systems serve to transport resources through-out the plant body. They also provide a structural support similar to a skeleton. Look closely at the mosses nearby and compare other visual differences.

Description: This species is limited to acidic wetlands with dense mosses and other organic matter. The horizontal stems ↑ are very slender and creep along the surface with occasional roots. Stems are variable in height from 1-5 inches tall. Leaves 0.25 inches long oriented to point upward. *Strobilus* looks like a bushy tail ↑ encompassing a third to a half of the upright stem.

Similar Species: Commonly overlooked, Bog Clubmoss might look a little like an infertile *Lycopodium*. If you are standing in a wetland, though, you can be mostly certain it's not *Lycopodium*. To be sure, look throughout the population for the absence of strobili on stalks.

clubmoss

Expanded tip of Bog Clubmoss resembles a bushy tail. Horizontal stem creeps across boggy surface. As its common name implies, this species grows in open bogs and fens.

Shining Firmoss *Huperzia lucidula*

clubmoss

Shady, cool, moist forests; occasionally on talus and rock ledges.

Nature Notes:

Huperzine is a chemical that may possibly be used in treatment of Alzheimers disease. This is one of the many natural chemicals in plants being studied to determine benefits for humans. One of the arguments for protecting the diversity of life on earth is that we don't yet know of possible health benefits the plant or animal may be to humans. We can add that to a longer list including oxygen production, carbon sequestration, ecological integrity and more. Why and how might you work to preserve the system of biological and non-biological components right before you at this very moment?

Formerly known as *Lycopodium lucidula.*

Very bristly, creeping, loosely clumped clubmoss.

Description: Bristly (sort of unkempt) looking plant with very distinct annual constrictions ↑. Growing in loose clumps (occasionally "fairy rings" as the older stems die back). The erect 6-8 inch tall stems are a continuation of the older stems that are often brownish and hiding under the leaf litter. Leaves are various in length, but less than 0.5 inches long with distinctly toothed edges ↑ and widest in the middle. *Sporangia* are in distinct zones on the upper stem ↑. *Gemmae* can be seen in one whorl ↑ on the end of upper stem.

Similar Species: Bristly Clubmoss and Common Clubmoss creep, but can be ruled out if you find sporangia in distinct zones on the upper portion of the stem. Rock Firmoss (*Huperzia porophila*) leaf edges are smooth and stomates can be found on the upper surface of the leaves while Shining Firmoss stomates are only on the lower surface of the leaves. You will need a hand lens for this.

clubmoss

Shining Firmoss show annual constrictions (top) and sporangia in distinct zones (bottom left). Gemmae are in one whorl at end of upper stem (top). In Rock Firmoss (*Huperzia porophila*) the stomates are on the upper surface of the leaves.

Rock Firmoss
Huperzia porophila

Rock Firmoss
Huperzia porophila

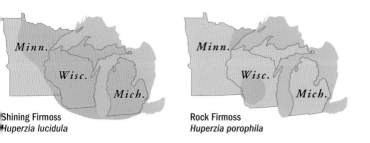

Shining Firmoss
Huperzia lucidula

Rock Firmoss
Huperzia porophila

Northern Firmoss *Huperzia selago*

Primarily in rocky, boreal forests in cool, damp sites.

Distinctly flat-topped tufted clubmoss primarily in rocky, boreal sites.

Nature Notes:

Unlike most *Huperzia*, Mountain Firmoss is determinate, which simply means that the whole plant dies after 12-15 years of spore production.

All *Huperzia* produce 3-lobed buds called gemmae that are dislodged and then take root in the soil below their parent. Spend a little time gently lifting some of the stems and plant litter to look for new growth. Look closely. What do you see?

Formerly known as *Lycopodium selago*.

Description: Low growing tufted ↑ plant (3-5 inches tall) with dense, small leaves (less than 0.25 inches). The leaves are smooth edged, narrow and pointed with stomates on both surfaces. Stem forks immediately at the base. Annual constrictions are barely noticeable. *Sporangia* are borne in distinct zones on upper stem ↑. *Gemmae* are often found in one whorl at the end of stems ↑—looks like a thick tip at the very end.

Similar Species: Mountain Firmoss (*Huperzia appressa*) is a bit smaller overall and the gemmae are numerous throughout the stems.

clubmoss

clubmoss

Mountain Firmoss
Huperzia appressa

Mountain Firmoss
Huperzia appressa

Northern Firmoss forms distinctly flat-topped tufts. Gemmae are in one whorl at end of stem; in Mountain Firmoss, gemmae are numerous throughout stem.

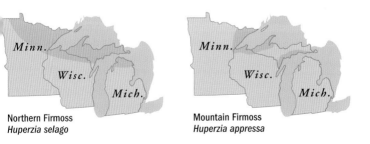

Northern Firmoss
Huperzia selago

Mountain Firmoss
Huperzia appressa

Prickly Tree Clubmoss *Dendrolycopodium dendroideum*

Acid soils of mixed forests and shrubby edge sites.

Upright branching tree-like clubmoss.

Nature Notes:

Dendroideum means tree-like. It certainly is "tree like" and common names include Princess Pine and Ground Pine even though they are far from being trees. Imagine the landscape when related species grew as tall as trees in a mature forest. During the Carboniferous Period, prior to dinosaurs, forests and even the air were much different than today.

Formerly *Lycopodium dendroideum*.

If you find some of these clubmosses in early Fall, lie down for a better perspective and tap the yellow strobili to watch spores fill the air.

Description: Relatively tall 12 inch stems arise every 6 inches from an underground stem with 4-5 branches in a tree-like form. *Strobili* are sessile ↑ and 1.5 inches long. As many as 1-7 strobili may be found per upright stem. The "trunk" has spreading, prickly leaves ↑. Leaves of branches are all equal in size. Common in rich hardwood forests.

Similar Species: Flat-branched Tree Clubmoss (*Dendrolycopodium obscurum*) and Hickey's Tree Clubmoss (*D. hickeyi*) are very similar in many respects. They can be immediately differentiated by the tightly appressed leaves on the "trunk." ↑ Flat-branched Tree Clubmoss has flat lateral branches ↑. The lateral branches of Hickey's Tree Clubmoss are round in cross section ↑ and this species is most often found in much drier, open sites.

clubmoss

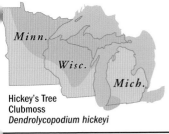

Flat-branched Tree Clubmoss
Dendrolycopodium obscurum

Hickey's Tree Clubmoss
Dendrolycopodium hickeyi

Prickly Tree Clubmoss has strobili that are sessile on upper stems (top right) and "trunk" with spreading, prickly leaves (middle right). Both *Dendrolycopodium obscurum* and *hickeyi* have a "trunk" with leaves tightly appressed; *obscurum* has lateral branches flat in cross section (bottom left inset) and *hickeyi* has lateral branches round in cross section (bottom right inset).

Prickly Tree
Clubmoss
Dendrolycopodium dendroideum

Hickey's Tree
Clubmoss
Dendrolycopodium hickeyi

Flat-branched
Tree Clubmoss
Dendrolycopodium obscurum

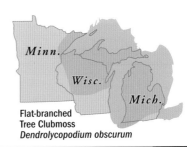

Northern Ground Cedar *Diphasiastrum complanatum*

clubmoss

Dry, open woods and rocky barrens.

Nature Notes:

Occasionally collected with greens for making Christmas wreaths, this and other artistically interesting lycopods may become locally at risk. As with any of our natural resources, it's imperative that we pay close attention to how we may use or even over-use the natural world around us.

Pay attention to the Latin names for hints as to how to identify them. I find it helpful to remember organisms' names by giving them human characteristics. For example, compare *D. digitatum* with *D. complanatum*. *D. complanatum* looks more complex with all of the branches apparently "messy" and interwoven. *D. digitatum*, on the other hand, is much more organized and put together like a proper southern gentlemen. How do you remember and notice the differences among species?

A cedar-like branching clubmoss.

Description: Shiny green tree-like clubmoss with flattened branches (scale-like leaves) at various angles (rebranched in irregular patterns) giving it an unkempt look. Horizontal stems are creeping on or very near the surface. Upright stems are as tall as 17 inches. The lateral branches have conspicuous constrictions ↑ marking the annual growth. Four-ranked leaves on stems. *Strobili* about 1 inch long atop long stalks (1.5-3 inches) that are sometimes forked with 1-2 per plant ↑.

Similar Species: Southern Ground Cedar (*Diphasiastrum digitatum*) has more orderly branches ↑ mostly horizontal to the forest floor and 2-4 strobili per stalk. Blue Ground Cedar (*D. tristachyum*) is a bit bluish-green ↑ overall with smaller strobili ↑ (0.5-1 inch long) and a very deep root system.

Southern Ground Cedar
Diphasiastrum digitatum

Blue Ground Cedar
Diphasiastrum tristachyum

Lateral branches are cedar-like and, hence, the common name of "ground cedar." Strobili at end of long forked stalk (top right). Northern Ground Cedar has "unkempt" branching pattern (opposite page), while Southern Ground Cedar shows a more orderly fan-shaped branching (bottom left).

Northern
Ground Cedar
Diphasiastrum complanatum

Blue Ground Cedar
Diphasiastrum tristachyum

Southern
Ground Cedar
Diphasiastrum digitatum

Blue Ground Cedar
Diphasiastrum tristachyum

clubmoss

Spikemosses

Spikemosses grow among true mosses of all kinds. They are easily over-looked. When you come across a rock outcrop, scan the surface for a slightly different color and texture. Our more common species, Rock Spikemoss, has a distinctly square cross-section that you will begin to see more readily as you run your fingers through their stems. Look closely, too, for the obvious yellow megaspores. Those megaspores are the female spores and they are located next to the main stem among the tiny leaves.

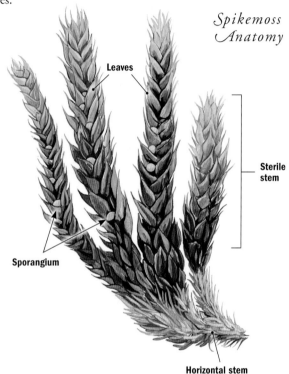

Spikemoss Anatomy

Leaves

Sterile stem

Sporangium

Horizontal stem

Quillworts

These might be the most surprising group included. Very few people are aware that we have pteridophytes growing under water. Wading in sandy streams or near the sandy shoreline of lakes and ponds will likely be enough to find them. If you are truly adventurous, grab a facemask and dive deep.

There are plenty of aquatic plants that look superficially similar. Though you shouldn't ignore the plants with leaves growing flat to the ground—they have feelings too—look for the distinctly tufted quill-like growth of the quillworts. There is no way around it, you'll have to dig your fingers into the sand to pull the entire plant up—roots and all.

With the plant in your hands, wash away any mud and debris so that you can look more closely. Peel away one leaf at a time until you begin to see tiny packets of cream-colored spores safely tucked at the base of a leaf. With your fingernail, scrape some spores out. Dry them for a few moments so that you can begin to see individual spores and then look at them closely under a hand lens. You will be looking for unique bumps and ridges to determine the species.

quillwort

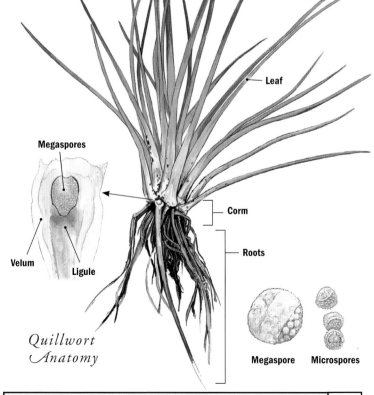

Leaf

Megaspores

Corm

Roots

Velum

Ligule

Quillwort Anatomy

Megaspore   Microspores

Rock Spikemoss *Selaginella rupestris*

In full sun on dry, open, siliceous rock outcrops.

A mat of grayish-green stiff moss-like stems.

Description: Small creeping gray-green plants often confused with mosses. As tall as 2 inches, the plant stems are rigid and distinctly 4-sided ↑ with yellowish megaspores ↑ scattered near the tips. The relatively thick leaves have toothed margins. They grow on rocky outcrops among mosses, grasses and sedges and can completely dry up and then rehydrate appearing to go from "dead" to "alive" in a single rainfall.

Similar Species: Northern Spikemoss (*Selaginella selaginoides*) is a very small creeping non-evergreen plant with upright fertile stems standing 2-5 inches tall. The strobilus is over 1 inch tall and cylindrical with yellowish-white megaspores. Sterile branches are prostrate. The thin leaves have toothed margins. Grows on cold lakeshores, talus slopes or spring-fed banks among mosses.

Nature Notes:

Often growing with *Polytrichum* mosses, this species lives on dry, often hot, hardened rock surfaces.

Rock Spikemoss will dry up and look a bit different when water is scarce and then quickly turn green and grow when water becomes available. Look around. What other plants do you see growing in the same niche and how do they appear to have adapted?

spikemoss

spikemoss

Northern Spikemoss
Selaginella selaginoides

Northern Spikemoss
Selaginella selaginoides

This species has distinctly 4-sided stems. Look for yellowish megaspores. Clumps of Rock Spikemoss can appear dry and even look dead. *Selaginella selaginoides* has very small creeping stems.

Rock Spikemoss
Selaginella rupestris

Northern Spikemoss
Selaginella selaginoides

Braun's Quillwort *Isoetes echinospora*

Freshwater ponds and slow-moving streams with sandy bottoms.

Small, circular arrangement of quill-like leaves.

Nature Notes:

The spores are borne in a pocket at the base of the older leaves. Isoetes have 2 types of spores: microspores are male and megaspores are female. Identification is very difficult and requires describing the ornamentation on megaspores that can be as large as 750 micrometers (the largest in the plant kingdom). Collect some on your finger. When enough moisture has evaporated, you'll begin to see some of the details. Either use a hand lens or take a closeup image with your camera. What do you see?

Description: Small (up to 9-18 inches tall) perennial aquatic rosette of quill-like leaves ↑ submerged in freshwater ponds (1-2 feet) or partially emergent in shallow low-nutrient ponds and slow-moving streams with sandy bottoms. The corm is often buried in mud. The leaves are unbranched and somewhat awl or quill-shaped. *Megaspores* observed with a 20x hand lens are covered with sharp spines ↑.

Similar Species: Lake Quillwort (*Isoetes lacustris*) most often grows deeply submerged (as much as 9 feet deep) in still, cool, low-nutrient lakes. Megaspores observed with a 20x hand lens are covered in crests with a distinct girdle of dense spines and ridges. Tends to be smaller overall—up to 9 inches tall.

quillwort

Lake Quillwort
Isoetes lacustris

Quillwort's rosette of quill-like leaves are found in sandy bottoms of freshwater ponds and slow streams. Spores are located at the base of leaves and have distinct ornamentation (top left).

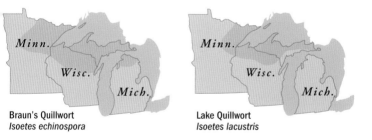

Braun's Quillwort
Isoetes echinospora

Lake Quillwort
Isoetes lacustris

Horsetails

Equisetum (horsetails and scouring rushes) is a great group to learn—of the 11 species in North America, 9 can be found in our area. Identification requires that you look closely at some basic structures: 1) presence or absence of the fertile "cone"; 2) presence or absence of branches; 3) shape, color and number of teeth at the nodes; 4) the relative size of the hollow in the main stem when compared to the thickness of the stem wall.

The fertile cones in some species will wither and fall away and so you may not see them. Generally speaking, branching occurs in horsetails. Lack of branches is an identifier of scouring rushes. There are exceptions and sometimes branches form late in a season or wither and fall away. Use a hand lens to examine the teeth at the nodes. Sometimes you will need to look at the nodes on the main stem and the branches. You won't always have to cut the plant to gain information about the hollow main stem—squeezing it between your fingers will often give you enough information.

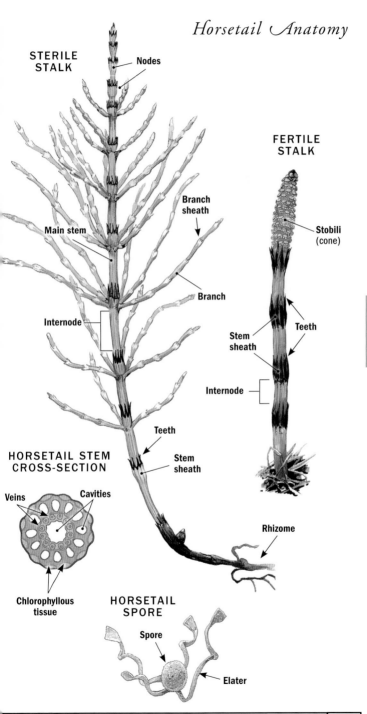

Horsetail Anatomy

STERILE STALK

Nodes

FERTILE STALK

Branch sheath

Main stem

Stobili (cone)

Branch

Internode

Teeth

Stem sheath

Internode

horsetails

Teeth

HORSETAIL STEM CROSS-SECTION

Stem sheath

Veins

Cavities

Rhizome

Chlorophyllous tissue

HORSETAIL SPORE

Spore

Elater

Field Horsetail   *Equisetum arvense*

Common in fields, roadsides and woods.

Nature Notes:

Often considered weedy, this is among our most common horsetails. They thrive in disturbed areas and spread easily on underground stems.

In early spring, be sure to look closely and notice when fertile stems poke out for the first time. Mark the date and keep close tabs. How long do they remain? What happens to them?

A highly variable and common bushy horsetail with simple stems often growing in dense clusters.

Description: Most common of the horsetails, it is often referred to as being weedy. The fertile stem (6-12 inches) appears early in the season and then withers and disappears a week or so later as the sterile stems begin to emerge. Fertile stem is pale brown and unbranched with 0.5 inch sheaths with large, dark, lance-shaped teeth. *Cone* is 1-1.5 inches long with blunt tip. The sterile stems are 6-24 inches tall, green, with 4-14 ridges; *sheaths* with small, dark brown teeth ↑ and white margins. Branches are in ascending whorls ↑ often with a bushy appearance. The central cavity of the main stem is very small

Similar Species: Meadow Horsetail (*Equisetum pratense*) is a very delicate, thin, simple-branching horsetail found in small,

Meadow Horsetail
Equisetum pratense

Meadow Horsetail
Equisetum pratense

horsetails

Fertile stem in early spring. Dense and bushy in some situations. Dark brown teeth with white margins; branches ascending. Meadow Horsetails' branches are distinctly horizontal.

scattered colonies in sunny meadows and wooded river edges often near springs and seeps. Whorled branches are distinctly horizontal ↑. The sheaths have 8-18 narrow sharp-pointed teeth (triangular) with dark brown centers and distinct white edges ↑. Central cavity is about one-third the diameter of the main stem.

Minn.

Wisc.

Mich.

Field Horsetail *Equisetum arvense*

Minn.

Wisc.

Mich.

Meadow Horsetail
Equisetum pratense

Water Horsetail *Equisetum fluviatile*

Common in sluggish water of rivers and ditches.

A smooth, hollow horsetail branching later in the season.

Nature Notes:

There seems to be more branching in shaded areas.

Fluviatile means "river."

Muskrats eat the young shoots.

Has been harvested for cattle feed.

Description: Smooth, hollow horsetail common in slow moving water. Green, erect, mostly solitary stems (14-48 inches tall) with hollow central cavity. Stems sometimes branching after cone forms. Branches are up to 6 inches long variable in length ↑. *Sheaths* wide, green with narrow black, sharp-pointed teeth ↑. *Cones* are 1 inch long and blunt tipped ↑ with short stem.

Similar Species: Much rarer to find, Marsh Horsetail (*Equisetum palustre*) is a slender branched horsetail growing solitary or in clusters. Stems usually with whorls of stout, upward curving branches growing 8-32 inches tall. Sheaths green, elongate, sometimes flared outward. Long narrow, pointed black teeth with white, rough margins. Branches hollow, 4-6 ridges. Central cavity of main stem is about 20 percent diameter. Cones are produced in mid-summer and have a blunt tip on a medium-short stem.

horsetails

Cones" blunt tipped. Variable branching later in the season. Narrow, sharp-pointed teeth.
central cavity hollow.

Marsh Horsetail
Equisetum palustre

Water
Horsetail
Equisetum fluviatile

Marsh
Horsetail
Equisetum palustre

Wood Horsetail *Equisetum sylvaticum*

Moist, shady forests and wooded swamps.

Nature Notes:

As with all of the *Equisetum*, close observation of the sheath teeth is also helpful for a positive identification. Look for the large, reddish teeth. It also helps to know how hollow the stem is or is not. I wonder, though, what are the adaptive advantages in both cases? Are there generalizations that can be made about the type of habitat and the resulting growth? Take note of your observations.

A common bright green, lacy branching horse-tail gracefully drooping at the tips.

Description: Fertile stems are 8 inches tall and first appear pale pink to brown without branches; branching and turning green after spores are discharged and the cone withers. Fertile stems are 10-27 inches tall; brownish to green. Mostly solitary. Slightly rough and hollow stems (about 33% of diameter). *Cone* one inch and rounded at tip with long stem disappearing in late spring ↑. *Teeth* reddish ↑, large and connected into 3-4 groups. *Branches* branch again ↑.

Similar Species: None of the other branching horsetails have compound branches— branches that rebranch. On early spring growth, look for the large, reddish sheath teeth of Wood Horsetail.

horsetails

Fertile stems (top right) emerge pale pinkish in spring, eventually sprouting branches and turning green. The "cone" withers in late spring (middle left). Teeth are reddish and large (middle right). Branches rebranch (bottom left). Stems wither and turn brown in fall (bottom right).

Tall Scouring Rush   *Equisetum hyemale*

Moist, sandy soils of woods, fields and shorelines.

Nature Notes:

Scouring Rush has been used to scour pots and pans. Before sandpaper was readily available, scouring rush was used in that place.

Classy violin builders still use this species during their final sanding of high-end violins. They simply slice open the plant stem lengthwise to make a bit of "sandpaper." The rough silica is imbedded in the plant fibers and does not come loose—as in manufactured sandpaper—leaving the fine pores of the wood unclogged. Try it on your next fine wood project.

Very tall, slender, hollow and non-branching dark green scouring rush.

Description: Tall, slender, hollow stems. Surfaces are rough with ash gray sheaths outlined above and below by dark edges ↑. Moist soils in woods, fields, sandy shores, etc. Grows 7-16 inches tall. Mostly unbranched. Fertile and sterile stems are alike. Sharp-pointed teeth usually wither and disappear quickly. *Cone* 0.5-1 inch long on short stem. The cone has a pointed tip ↑ and matures in summer. *Internodes* often bulge with age. Central cavity is 66 percent of stem diameter.

Similar Species: Smooth Scouring Rush (*Equisetum laevigatum*) is very hard to distinguish. Look for blunt cones and a distinct black band at the top of each slightly flared sheath. It also tends to appear paler green and more fragile than Tall Scouring Rush.

horsetails

The pointed tip "cones" mature in summer (bottom left). Teeth are usually absent from sheaths; sheaths ash-gray. Stems hollow.

Tall Scouring Rush
Equisetum hymale

Smooth Scouring Rush
Equisetum laevigatum

Variegated Scouring Rush *Equisetum variegatum*

Cool, shady spots along stream banks; occasionally in sunny ditches.

Nature Notes:

Humans identify various species based upon predictable visual structures, colors, etc. This is true for this species too, but the very name captures the fact that this species is defined by its varying colors. Why not have multiple species here that could capture each variation? A species is defined not by external looks, but by reproductive results. Similarly, dogs vary dramatically from one to another while they are all the same species.

A very slender, dark green scouring rush growing in twisted tufts of dense colonies.

Description: Rare. Very slender, dark green species seldom branching. It grows in twisted tufts. *Sheaths* over cones are black and white (variegated) ↑. *Stems* 3-19 inches tall. Rough with small central cavity. *Cone* small, greenish with short stem and sharp-pointed tip ↑; matures late summer and overwinters to disperse spores in spring. Distinct black and white *sheaths* ↑ with persistent teeth.

Similar Species:

Presence of the sharply pointed cone, distinctly variegated sheaths and persistent sheath teeth make it likely that you won't mistake this species.

horsetails

Newly forming cone

Mature cone

Spores have released, cone withers

This scouring rush is distinctly colored

horsetails

"Cones" are sharp-pointed and small. Distinct black and white sheath teeth are the reason this species common name is "Variegated." Often found in dense colonies.

Minn.

Wisc.

Mich.

Dwarf Scouring Rush *Equisetum scirpoides*

Often hidden among the leaf litter in moist mixed forests.

Nature Notes:

Scirpoides means "resembling *Scirpus*." *Scirpus* is a flowering plant in the genus of sedges having common names such as clubrush and bulrush. Though they do have some resemblance, you won't mistake them once you have a working familiarity with this species. And that is true of most things in our lives, isn't it? It takes time to truly get to know a species. Take some time today and get to know this species.

Very small curling ↑, wiry stems forming dense colonies.

Description: Smallest of the *Equisetum* species. Black sharp-pointed cones grow at tips. Forest species of cool areas, rare and local. About 1-8 inches tall. *Teeth* form a dark band on the sheath. No central cavity. *Cones* mature in summer and overwinter to disperse in early spring. Each stem node has 3 teeth ↑.

Similar Species: No similar species. Both the small size and curling habit distinguish this species quite easily.

horsetails

Tiny cones overwinter. Teeth form dark bands ringing the sheath. Clusters of Dwarf Scouring Rush look like a mass of small curling, wiry stems.

Minn.

Wisc.

Mich.

Moonworts

You will first need to assume the appropriate position—on hands and knees in a "botrychulating" posture. It's true! "Botrychulating" requires great patience. Move slowly and pick through the grasses, mosses and leaves of other plants to discover the magic of moonworts and grape-ferns.

In newer taxonomy, three genera divide all of the *Botrychium* included in this guide. Reference the appendix for the variety of new names if you wish. The newer taxonomy in the next few paragraphs demonstrates some of the distinct differences that you will see.

Moonworts (*Botrychium*) are tiny and sort of short-lived. Both the sporophore and tropophore arise on one main stalk from the ground. Look closely at the general shape and divisions on the tropophore. Sporophores might be divided with many or a few branches and, even though it arises above the tropophore, it might be shorter or longer than the spore-bearing stem. When you see one, you may see more of the same and also a variety of other species. Keep looking.

Grapeferns (*Sceptridium*) are a bit larger and generally longer lasting. The sporophore and tropophore arise from the ground on separate stems. Look at the edges of the tropophore for comparison among species.

Rattlesnake Fern (*Botrypus*) is our largest and most common of the members in this group. At first sight it may look like a small, fleshy Bracken Fern. You will notice the sporophore emerging from the triangular tropophore and also a slight pink in the stipe.

This group also includes the difficult to find Adder's Tongue (*Ophioglossum*). Like those above, it can live many years simply growing underground until conditions are right. Adder's Tongue leaves are smooth and simple. They often grow among grasses and can be right in front of you almost invisible. This rare treat is worth the effort. Put it high on your list.

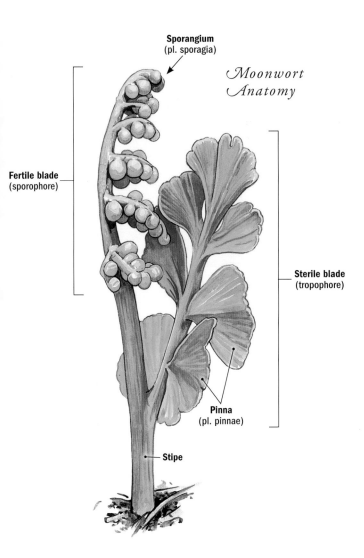

Sporangium
(pl. sporagia)

Moonwort
Anatomy

Fertile blade
(sporophore)

Sterile blade
(tropophore)

moonwort

Pinna
(pl. pinnae)

Stipe

Northern Adder's Tongue *Ophioglossum pusillum*

Sandy open swamps, marsh edges, grassy pastures, old fields and roadside ditches.

Nature Notes:

Ophioglossum has 1262 chromosomes packed into each cell—the highest count of any known living organism. In contrast, humans have 46 chromosomes and the ant, *Myrmecia pilosula*, has only 2 chromosomes.

It can go completely dormant during dry years and then rise above the soil surface in years with favorable conditions.

Named by early herbalists because of the similarity to a snake tongue.

Pusillum refers to "very small."

Rarely noticed, the single leaf looks more like a lily or orchid leaf.

Description: Growing only about 2-8 inches tall, Adder's Tongue has a single light green sterile *blade* ↑ that is widest at the midpoint. The sterile blade is about 4 inches long at most, erect and soft. The *sporophore* might be about 2-5 inches above the height of the sterile blade. The *sporangia bearing portion* is about 1-2 inches long and bears 10-40 pairs of sporangia ↑ coming to a narrow tip.

Similar Species: The blade looks much like a lily or orchid leaf, but it has netted veins and lacks a midvein.

Sporangia grouped in 10 to 40 pairs. Sterile blade smooth and lacking veins. Plant resembles some *Malaxis* orchids, which are also found in the North Woods, but notice this moonwort's netted leaf vein which lacks a midvein.

Common Moonwort   *Botrychium lunaria*

Dry meadows, hillsides, rocky ledges under Northern White Cedar, roadsides, cliffs or dunes.

Nature Notes:

Moonwort is associated with many myths as a magical plant known to unshoe horses, unlock safes, raise the dead and cure lunacy. It is so tiny and difficult to locate, it just might drive you loony looking for it.

Common Moonwort often grows mixed with other *Botrychium* and will hybridize. In the 1950s and 60s, Warren H. and Florence S. Wagner published a series of studies showing that ferns and other plants hybridize freely, regularly leading to new species. University of Michigan professors, the Wagners made major contributions to our knowledge of *Botrychium* especially in the 1980s and 90s.

Very tiny fern with shiny, deep green fan-shaped leaves.

Description: Often under 6 inches tall, the sterile blade is divided into 6 or more pairs of shiny, deep green fan-shaped pinnae growing very closely together and often overlapping ↑. The sterile blade (2-4 inches long and 1-2 inches wide) emerges from the common stipe about hallway up the length of entire plant. *Pinnae* are half moon-shaped with somewhat wavy margins ↑. *Veins* spread like the ribs of a fan. *Sporophore* 1-5 inches long with branching clusters ↑ bending lightly downward.

Similar Species: Common Moonwort's sterile blade is sessile to the stipe and the half-moon shaped pinnae overlap each other. These characteristics set it apart from other moonworts.

moonwort

Fan-shaped pinnae of Common Moonwort often overlap. The sporophore has branching clusters.

moonwort

Least Moonwort   *Botrychium simplex*

Damp meadows, moist woods, edges of pastures and roads.

Nature Notes:

Least Moonwort barely emerges above leaf litter and remains dormant during dry years.

Non-native earthworms are a major conservation issue in our forests. Introduced from Europe, these worms quickly consume soil organics. Mooworts suffer the consequences. Can you see worm damage in your forests?

Spores of most *Botrychium* must be washed deep into the soil and total darkness for successful germination. Some theorize that spores of Least Moonwort must also pass through a small mammal gut.

Very tiny, simple moonwort.

Description: Very tiny Moonwort only 2-7 inches tall; often about the size of your thumb The sterile blade is 0.5-3 inches long, ascending and appears to clasp the stalk. Smooth, fleshy, pale green with 1-3 pairs of rounded pinnae ↑. The common stalk is about 1 inch long, fleshy, smooth, pale green. *Sporophore* is often unbranched ↑, long stalked and usually overtops the sterile blade. *Sporangia* small but prominent and widely spaced. *Basal pinnae* are usually larger than second pair.

Similar Species: Little Goblin Moonwort (*Botrychium mormo*) is an extremely small and secretive yellow-green moonwort of rich Sugar Maple, Beech and Basswood forests. A very succulent moonwort that produces a 2 inch long sterile blade with very short, squarish pinnae ↑. Sporangia are tightly appressed to the stalk ↑.

Least Moonwort is very tiny with 1-3 pairs of rounded pinnae. Sporophore usually overtops the blade.

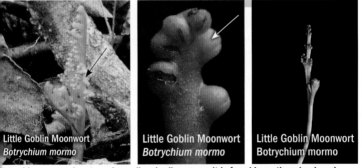

Little Goblin Moonwort
Botrychium mormo

Little Goblin Moonwort
Botrychium mormo

Little Goblin Moonwort
Botrychium mormo

Botrychium mormo is extremely small and yellow-green. It is found in northern hardwood forests

Least
Moonwort
Botrychium simplex

Little Goblin
Moonwort
Botrychium mormo

moonwort

Pale Moonwort *Botrychium pallidum*

Open sandy fields, gravel ridges and marshy lakeshores.

Nature Notes:

All *Botrychium* require an association with a mycorrhizal symbiont of the genus *Glomus*. The ferns can remain dormant for many years as they receive carbon from their mycorhizal partner. Pale Moonwort and Prairie Moonwort are unique in that they produce masses of gemmae (small buds able to grow into new plants) on underground stems. The gemmae serve as a form of asexual propogation.

Very small, waxy, pale green moonwort.

Description: Small (1-3 inches long) waxy, pale green herbaceous frond. Sterile blade with 5 pairs of fan-shaped ↑ pinnae folded inwards with entire margins. *Sporangia* sometimes present on lobes of lower pinnae ↑.

Similar Species: Prairie Moonwort (*Botrychium campestre*) tends to have a more succulent blade and seems to prefer drier habitats. Its pinnae are mostly linear. Spoon-leaf Moonwort (*B. spathulatum*) grows in fields and inland dunes in Michigan and has spoon-shaped pinna that do not overlap. Mingan Moonwort (*B. minganense*) grows in grassy meadows and older maple forests. Its pinnae are fan-shaped.

moonwort

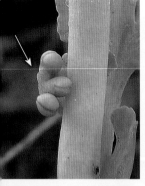

Prairie Moonwort *Botrychium campestre*

Sporangia sometimes present on lower pinnae (top left). The "pale" in Pale Moonwort refers to its light green, fan-shaped pinnae (bottom left). Pinnae details are important to notice when identifying *Botrychium*.

moonwort

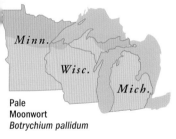

Pale Moonwort
Botrychium pallidum

Mingan Moonwort
Botrychium minganese

Spoon-leaf Moonwort
Botrychium spathulatum

Prairie Moonwort
Botrychium campestre

Daisy-leaf Moonwort   *Botrychium matricariifolium*

Edges of rich moist forests, old fields, roadsides, dunes and in areas with sparse grass cover.

Nature Notes:

While exploring older logging roads or gravel pits, keep a sharp eye out along the edges for small patches of strawberry mixed with a few hawkweed and sedges. Set your pack down and assume the moonwort position—on your hands and knees. That's right. If you are going to find moonworts, you need to dedicate focused time searching very closely and slowly.

Most common moonwort with pale green, daisy-like leaves.

Description: It is a stout 2-10 inches tall with a pale green sterile blade shaped somewhat like daisy leaves ↑. The blade is 0.5-4 inches long, erect, stalked, with 2-7 pairs of narrow, rounded pinnae that are deeply lobed. The common *stipe* is 1-8 inches tall, slender, fleshy, pale, chalky green, often with a pink stripe. *Sporophore* is erect with 3 large branches ↑ bearing small clusters of yellow, obvious *sporangia*. The sporophore branch is often longer than the sterile blade.

Similar Species: Triangle Moonwort (*B. lanceolatum*) grows in moist, cool, rich forests in humus-rich soil among Sugar Maple; sometimes among Northern White Cedar swamps. The leaf blade is nearly sessile. Sporophore is 3 branched. Sporangia are bright greenish yellow. Releases spores later than other moonworts.

Triangle Moonwort
Botrychium lanceaolatum

Named for its distinctly daisy-like leaves. Sporophore with 3 large branches (top middle and right). *Botrychium lanceolatum* has a leaf blade that is nearly sessile (bottom right).

Daisy-leaf Moonwort
Botrychium matricariifolium

Triangle Moonwort
Botrychium lanceolatum

moonwort

Leathery Grapefern *Botrychium multifidum*

Rocky, poor soils and blueberry barrens.

moonwort

Nature Notes:

In early summer you can find both the old and new sterile blades side by side (one limp and the other lush and lively). It's possible to find all of our Grapeferns growing together in small, mixed populations. If you find one species, continue to look closely for others. Rugulose Grapefern (*B. rugulosum*) grows in sandy soils of pastures reverting back to woodlands and sometimes under Staghorn Sumac and among Jack Pine and Red Pine.

Leathery and succulent low growing grapefern.

Description: Very leathery and succulent shiny green to grayish green leaves. Sterile blade is 2-6 inches long and equally wide. Broadly triangular and horizontal to the ground. There are 3-5 pairs of *pinnae* each on long stalks with the lowest pairs the largest. *Pinnules* often overlapping ↑ with rounded tips and entire margins. *Sporophore* wide spreading ↑, branching, prominent and taller than the sterile blade with many *sporangia*.

Similar Species: Rugulose Grapefern (*Botrychium rugulosum*) has thin sterile blades about 6-12 inches long and wide. They are divided into numerous pinnae with trowel-shaped pinnules that have coarse toothed margins. Blunt-lobed Grapefern (*B. oneidense*) are also very similar, but with blunt-tipped pinnules ↑ and very finely toothed margins.

Rugulose Grapefern
*Botrychium
rugulosum*

Top left image shows leaves in spring after a winter under the snow. Leathery, way-edged pinnules. Sporophore separate and taller than blade.

Leathery
Grapefern
Botrychium multifidum

Blunt-lobed
Grapefern
Botrychium oneidense

Rugulose
Grapefern
Botrychium rugulosum

moonwort

Dissected Grapefern *Botrychium dissectum*

Dry and moist woods, fields, floodplains and sandy areas.

Nature Notes:

Also known as Cut-leaved Grapefern.

The blades appear in summer and last through winter into the next spring turning bronze after a frost in fall.

Sometimes grows among thick patches of *Polytrichum* mosses.

Botrychium is a Greek word used in reference to a cluster of grapes.

Most *Botrychium* are disturbance-adapted plants able to colonize short-lived habitats—often disturbed areas with little plant cover.

Leathery and lacy-cut grapefern.

Description: Variable species. The semi-leathery, coarse, fleshy, triangular sterile blade diverges from the sporophore at or below the ground surface. The sterile blade is 8-12 inches long and wide. It appears divided into 3 sections with basal pinnae much larger. *Pinnae* are trowel-shaped, often divided into pinnules with toothed or lacy-cut edges ↑ with pointed tips. Grows on a stalk 1-7 inches tall. *Sporophore* is 2-8 inches long and overtops the sterile blade. The branched light yellow *sporangia* wither soon after spores release in late summer.

Similar Species: Though all of our grapeferns (*B. multifidum, B. rugulosum, B. oniedense* and *B. dissectum*) have a similar overall growth pattern, Dissected Grapefern stands out as the most toothed and lacy-cut.

moonwort

Note the very finely cut leaves that give this grapefern its common name. The sporophore is separate and taller than blade. Sporangia are yellowish and on branching stalks (right).

Rattlesnake Fern *Botrychium virginianum*

Moist deciduous forests and shady woodlands.

Nature Notes:

The largest and most common *Botrychium* in North America.

Called "Rattlesnake Fern" because when it first opens the sporangia-bearing tip resembles a rattlesnake tail. The mashed roots were also apparently used by Native Americans as a treatment for snake bites.

Common in groups, if you see one, you will likely be able to find many others secretly "hiding" nearby.

Mid-sized, three-parted ↑ bright green fern with a distinct upright fertile stem overtopping the frond.

Description: Bright yellow-green triangular and much dissected sterile blade horizontal to the ground. The *blade* is 4-12 inches long and wide. *Pinnae* are narrowly cut into pinnules that are toothed, lobed or cut; up to 12 pairs on large plants. *Veins* are few and simple. The *stipe* is 4-8 inches long below the blade; smooth ↑, fleshy, round and pinkish at base. *Sporophore* is spreading and ascending atop a slender stalk that rises above the sterile blade ↑. *Sporangia* are bright yellow withering after early summer.

Similar Species: Smaller versions of Rattlesnake Fern might be confused with some of the larger, more triangular moonworts. Look for the pinkish stipe in Rattlesnake Fern.

moonwort

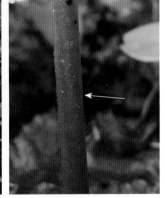

moonwort

Rattlesnake Fern is a very large triangular, three-parted *Botrychium*. Sporophore distinctly overtops the frond. The stipe is smooth and fleshy and pinkish at base (bottom right).

Ferns of Forests

Most of our obvious ferns grow in forests. For the purposes of this guide, the "forests" of this section have dry to moist soils. If you are obviously in a swamp, have damp or muddy shoes or feel a squishiness below you, turn to *Ferns of Wet Areas*. This can be hard to judge sometimes. All of our ferns need moisture and will thrive in moist soil if able to compete. If you don't find your fern in the Ferns of Wet Areas, come back to this section.

Often, you can expect to find forest ferns growing in distinct colonies or clumps. While working to identify the species, look at the others in the area to see overall variety for form and to also find fertile fronds.

Before perusing the pages that follow, it's helpful to take note of the height of the fern, the nearby forest plant species and the shape and location of sporangia. Also take note of any hairs, scales or other unique qualities of the rachis.

Ferns of Wet Areas

Forested and open wetlands are included here. Sometimes you'll find obvious clumps and dense growth of a particular fern. Other times, you may only find a single fern growing among the mosses. There are likely other individuals nearby hiding among the vegetation. Sometimes, the phenology of an area may be far behind others due to drier conditions or a colder substrate. Dig your hand deep into the sphagnum moss of a fen or bog in early summer and you may find ice below.

"Wet Areas" is also a highly variable term. You might find Royal Fern emerging from knee-deep water in one place and from a barely moist mossy dip in the forest floor in another. Also, you may find Braun's Holly Fern growing in the extreme primary branches of a rocky stream. During drier times, those same little rivulets may appear as a marginally eroded landscape. I have found the Braun's Holly Fern growing in the middle of a busy hiking trail that appeared poorly managed. Fortunately, trail maintenance has been halted there—an "improved" trail most certainly would have damaged the apparently thriving population.

Ferns of Rocky Areas

Everyone has a favorite habitat; I love rocky outcrops, talus slopes and cliff faces. All the species in this section are at once extremely hardy and tenderly fragile. Just as this hard surface can crumble and fall away, so can the ferns that grow here. Be careful. Take light steps. If you are a rock climber, use proper climbing ethics and leave no trace.

In some instances, you may search year after year and never find some of these species like the Maidenhair Spleenwort and some rare Cliff Ferns. In others, you may notice that they are only very localized but seem to be very common in that small area as will be the case for Fragrant Fern and Slender Cliff Brake. Still, as with the Smooth Cliff Brake and Fragile Fern, you may find a little tuft magically emerging from a crevice that seems impossible to colonize.

Most all of the species in the rocky areas of the North Woods are very distinct. Once you see most of them, they are fairly easy to identify. Some *Woodsia*, on the other hand, will require very close observation of some minute characteristics that will require patience and a hand lens.

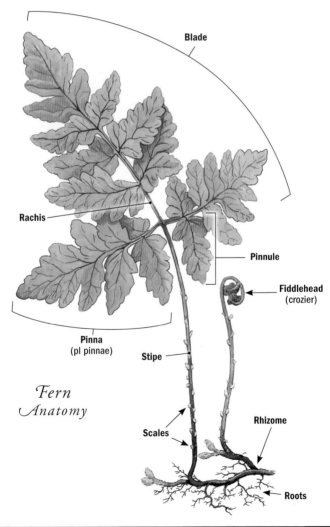

Blade

Rachis

Pinnule

Fiddlehead
(crozier)

Pinna
(pl pinnae)

Stipe

*Fern
Anatomy*

Scales

Rhizome

Roots

Eastern Bracken Fern *Pteridium aquilinum*

Varied forests but most often in drier, sunny open areas with sandy soils.

Nature Notes:

This genus has only one species (divided into two subspecies and 12 varieties) very common across several continents.

The crozier forms in 3 sections and looks like an eagle's claw giving it the name *aquilinum* for "eagle." (photo bottom left of opposite page.)

Produces new fronds throughout summer.

In the 17th century they burned it to bring rain to dry farm fields. In myth, smoke from the burning fronds also drove away snakes, gnats and "other noisome creatures." The ash was then used as a fertilizer. Deep rhizomes make this species fire resistant overall.

Very common, knee to waist high three-parted fern growing in dense colonies.

Description: Strong, knee-high three-part ↑ fern growing in dense colonies in many, varied habitats. *Fronds* 3 feet tall. *Blade* is about 2 feet wide divided into 3 parts and very triangular; almost parallel to the ground and leathery. *Pinnae* are longer than wide. *Stipe* long and about same length as blade; smooth and rigid with grooved, square corners. Spreads most commonly from a dark, scaleless rhizome about 1 inch thick and often 15 feet long (very cord-like). *Sori* form infrequently in narrow lines near margins and covered partially by the reflexed edges.

Similar Species: The margins, lower surface and costa have hairs in variety *latiusculum*; mostly hairless in variety *pseudocaudatum* (a much more southerly species). Similar 3-parted ferns are much smaller and won't be confused.

forests

Distinctly three-parted fern. Brackens commonly grow in dense colonies. They begin yellowing in late summer. The fiddlehead (crozier) reminded an early naturalist of an "eagle's claw" (bottom left); this is how this fern got its specific epithet *aquilinum,* which contains the Latin root of "eagle." Three-parted stem is a good identifier (bottom right).

Minn.

Wisc.

Mich.

Northern Maidenhair Fern *Adiantum pedatum*

Rich, deciduous forests and sometimes on rocky slopes.

Nature Notes:

Stipes have been used in basketry.

Adiantum in general was once used as a cure for baldness—likely as a result of the Doctrine of Signatures in that the fern looked like a maiden's long hair.

Adiantum is derived from the Greek *adiantos* which means "unmoistened."

The leaves repel water and appear to stay dry.

Pedatum refers to the decreasing outward growth pattern seen in our toes.

A very graceful fern with more or less horizontal fan-shaped blades often forming small colonies.

Description: Very graceful, somewhat arching blades in a more or less horizontal manner. Fronds 16-26 inches tall. *Blades* are fan-shaped. *Rachis* and *stipe* are smooth and black to purple-brown ↑. *Rhizome* is creeping with grayish brown scales near the growing portion. *False indusium* formed by inrolled *pinnule* margin ↑. *Croziers* are wine red, delicate and emerge early in spring ↑.

Similar Species: Two similar species not found in the North Woods (yet): Western Maidenhair Fern (*A. aleuticum*), found in disjunct locations as far east as Maine, will have more erect or vertical fronds. Southern Maidenhair Fern (*A. capillus-veneris*), located as far north as Missouri, does not have a forked stipe.

forests

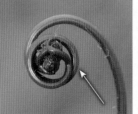

Leaf margins are very distinctive (top). Commonly in dense colonies. Stipes smooth and black to purple-brown (top right). The developing fern fiddlehead (crozier) is wine red (bottom left). Maidenhair may still be bright green even after the leaves have fallen.

Minn.

Wisc.

Mich.

forests

Interrupted Fern *Osmunda claytoniana*

Drier, rich, shaded woods and meadows.

Nature Notes:

Among our oldest living fern species dating back to 210 million years ago, the Interrupted Fern remains one of the few species still existing today that also existed among dinosaurs.

Consider this for a moment— the average fossil record for flowering plants is about 3-5 million years and *Homo sapiens* arose only about 2 million years ago. Interrupted Fern has remained unchanged and very successful more than 100 times longer than the human species.

A large, clump-forming fern with withered brownish fertile structures distinctly "interrupting" the entire fronds.

Description: Large, clumping arched fern interspersed with some fronds that have distinct interruptions ↑ along the rachis forming withered brownish structures ↑ that are actually modified fertile *pinnae*. *Fronds* can grow up to 5 feet long with a yellowish *stipe*. Fertile fronds are taller and more erect; sterile fronds are smaller and arching. *Pinnae* deeply cut into oval, semi-overlapping lobes. *Rachis* is smooth, green with a groove in front. *Rhizomes* are very stout and creeping with stubble remnants obviously visible in late fall.

Similar Species: It is very possible to confuse this with Cinnamon Fern. Look first for at least one frond in the clump that contains fertile pinnae "interrupting" the other pinnae. Also, note the ground surrounding you—if it's relatively dry you are likely looking at an infertile clump of Interrupted Fern.

forests

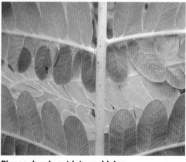

Pinnae deeply cut into oval lobes.
Frond distinctly interrupted by fertile pinnae
(main photo on opposite page).
Stout, creeping rhizomes obvious in late fall.

"Interrupting" fertile pinnae

Minn.

Wisc.

Mich.

forests

Northern Lady Fern *Athyrium filix-femina*

Moist woods, swamps and fields.

Nature Notes:

Filix-femina means "female fern" and might refer to the ancient belief that this was the diminutive female version of the Male Fern (*Dryopteris filix-mas*). It may also refer to the graceful appearance.

One form of Lady Fern has distinctly red stems. It was once known as variety *rubellum*, but is now simply a color form.

Spend some time looking around and you might see distinct patterns of these color forms across the landscape. What might the patterns be related to?

Very common large, showy fern with lacy-cut fronds growing in circular clumps.

Description: *Fronds* are 1.5-3 feet long, lanceolate with very narrow pointed tips. *Pinnae* are short without a stalk. No hairs on the blade and pointed teeth lack bristle tips. *Pinnules* cut to midvein of pinnae and deeply toothed. *Rachis* is pale, smooth with a few hairs or scales. *Stipe* is greenish red with scattered brown scales ↑ and the base is often dark brown/black. *Rhizome* is very scaly, creeping, branching with many old stalks still attached. *Sori* elongate, straight to horseshoe shaped. *Spores* are yellow.

Similar Species: Silvery Spleenwort (pg. 90) have lobed pinnules, rather than cut and toothed in Lady Fern. New York Ferns (pg. 92) lack toothed margins. Wood Ferns tend to have much larger lower pinnae.

forests

Look closely at lowermost pinnae; inner pinnules are large above.
Brown scales on a green stipe (bottom right). Distinctly red stems found in some color forms (bottom middle).
Brown and withering in fall (bottom left).

forests

Silvery Spleenwort *Deparia acrostichoides*

Damp woods and shaded slopes.

Tall, soft green fern with silvery sori and hairs that give an overall pale sheen.

Nature Notes:

Also known as Silvery Glade Fern

Occasionally used as an indicator species, Silvery Spleenwort is associated with high diversity habitats of headwater streams in Maple forests.

Find this species and you will likely be among a variety of other less common species (including varied difficult to identify sedges and grasses) dependent upon a narrow range of needs. Forest managers should take note of these communities and make appropriate plans to protect them.

Description: *Fronds* 12-13 inches long and 5-10 inches wide. Fertile fronds taller and more slender appear in late summer. Blade tapering at both ends. Silvery hairs common along costae and veins. Lowest pair of *pinnae* point downward. *Pinnules* not cut to midvein, finely toothed edges. *Rachis* pale green and hairy ↑. Groove of costa not connected to groove on rachis. *Stipe* usually much shorter than blade and has long white hairs until late summer. *Rhizome* black and creeping. *Sori* narrow, long, straight in a herringbone pattern.

Similar Species: Very similar overall to Lady Fern (pg. 88) but the pinnae are lobed in *Deparia* instead of toothed. Also, Lady Ferns are often clumped, while *Deparia* are loosely clustered.

forests

Rachis with soft, whitish hairs (top). Stipe shorter than blade with whitish hairs. Sori in herringbone pattern.

Minn.

Wisc.

Mich.

forests

New York Fern *Thelypteris noveboracensis*

Woods and thickets especially under gaps in the forest canopy or on the edges of swamps or streams.

Nature Notes:

New York Fern can be found in sunny patches resulting from gaps in the forest canopy that are near temporary wet areas or streams and swamps. As deciduous tree canopies expand, the fern's potential for success decreases. In an apparent "fair play" response, the dense canopy of New York Fern fronds actually deters tree seedling growth and survivorship. Ferns canopies?! The next time you enter a fern "forest," drop low to the ground to see a canopy of ferns.

Yellow-green mid-sized fern growing in colonies

Description: *Frond* tapers at both ends and i about 8-25 inches long in tufts of 3 or more on a rhizome. Delicate blade tapers from middle at both ends. Finely hairy beneath. *Pinnae* long pointed ↑, narrow and cut nearly to mid-vein in rounded lobes. *Rachis* green, pale and often smooth ↑. *Rhizome* dark brown, widely creeping producing fronds in tufts. *Sori* few, round, small, near margins. *Indusium* pale tan

Similar Species: Hay-scented Fern (*Dennstaedtia punctilobula*) forms extensive colonies in rows along their rhizomes while New York Ferns tend to grow in clumps of 3 or more fronds.

forests

Hay-scented Fern
Dennstaedtia punctilobula

Frond tapers at both ends (top left). Pinnae long pointed and deeply cut.
Rachis green and often smooth (top right).

New York Fern
Thelypteris noveboracensis

Hay-scented Fern
Dennstaedtia punctilobula

forests

Spinulose Wood Fern *Dryopteris carthusiana*

Swamps, moist woods and slopes.

Nature Notes:

Many ferns readily hybridize. Spinulose Wood Fern is a fertile tetraploid. What does that mean? Most hybrids are infertile—you will know this if you find irregularly shaped spores. Tetraploid describes having four sets of chromosomes rather than the two sets you might expect in many plants and animals. Spores are typically haploid (just one set of chromosomes) and form diploid plants when the two sets of parent chromosomes come together.

Relatively common larger, lacy, clump-forming fern.

Description: *Fronds* 8-30 inches; 4-12 inches wide. *Blade* mostly triangular; nearly the same width at base and middle. *Pinnae* often angled upward; on the lower pinna, lowest *pinnules* next to rachis usually longest; fine-toothed margins ↑ with bristle tips that curve inward. *Rachis* is green with scattered pale brown scales ↑. *Stipe* often shorter than blade with pale brown scales. *Rhizome* thick, coarse, creeping. *Sori* are small and situated midway between midvein and margin. *Indusium* kidney-shaped.

Similar Species: Northern Wood Fern (*Dryopteris expansa*) is an obviously lacy fern of cool, moist woods and rocky slopes. Fronds to 3 feet, not evergreen, wider at base than most other *Dryopteris*. Stipe scaly at base. Pinnules on lower pinna nearest rachis are "apparently" missing ↑ and the next pair are very large (often 2-3x size of upper pinnule).

forests

Spinulose Wood Fern
Dryopteris carthusiana

Northern Wood Fern
Dryopteris expansa

Notice the innermost pinnules on lowest pinnae, which are longer than adjacent pinnule. Fine-toothed margins with curved bristles. Stipe with pale brown scales. *Dryopteris expansa* has distinct gap between the rachis and the lowermost pinnules (bottom right).

forests

Spinulose Wood Fern
Dryopteris carthusiana

Northern Wood Fern
Dryopteris expansa

Male Fern *Dryopteris filix-mas*

Cool, moist woods and shaded talus slopes.

Nature Notes:

Early botanist thought that this robust fern was the male version of the Lady Fern. Knowledge of reproduction in ferns was lacking. In fact, it was once commonly thought that all plants reproduced with seeds; fern "seeds" were simply invisible.

On June 23 of each year, people would make attempts to capture the seed believing that they would also capture the magic of invisibility. The lore of ferns is filled with magic and mystery.

Uncommon, large, dark green fern forming distinct upright crowns.

Description: *Fronds* 10-40 inches long, widest about 1/3 up from base and cut into 20 pairs of pinnae. *Pinnae* are narrow, long pointed cut almost to midvein with rounded lobes and slightly toothed margins. *Rachis* green and scaly beneath. *Stipe* is 4 inches long; grooved and densely covered with two kinds of light brown scales (one broad and one hari-like). *Sori* are large, prominent ↑, between midvein and margin on upper half of blade. On lower *pinna* the first *pinnule* is larger than the second.

Similar Species: Marginal Wood Fern (pg. 100) are more leathery and have sori on the margins.

forests

Male Ferns form distinctly upright crowns. Their sori are large and prominent on back of the blades.

Evergreen Wood Fern *Dryopteris intermedia*

Moist to dry rocky woods with rich soils.

Nature Notes:

Also known as Fancy Fern.

This is not an evergreen fern, as the name implies. Actually, the previous year's growth holds on to the green through the winter and can be used as a diagnostic feature even into the summer. Eventually the dead fronds will give up their green and wither away as the canopy leafs out. They don't last forever and might better be termed "winter green." How long do you notice them lasting?

Medium to large semi-arching lacy fern in upright circular clusters with the previous year's dead (but still mostly green) fronds lying at the base ↑.

Description: *Fronds* 1-3 feet long; 4-10 inches wide; seemingly evergreen. The *blade* has glandular hairs on *rachis* and *costa*. Look at the innermost *pinnules* (closest to rachis) of basal pinnae and you'll notice they are slightly shorter than the adjacent pinnules on same side of costa ↑. There is a medial dark stripe on the *stipe* that is a quarter of the frond length with light brown scales at base. *Rhizome* is thick, coarse and scaly. Small *sori* are arranged between midvein and margin ↑.

Similar Species: Many other *Dryopteris* species can be confused. Compare the innermost pinnules of the basal pinnae and look for persistently green fronds lying at the base.

forests

Notice that the innermost pinnules on the lowest pinnae are shorter than adjacent pinnule (top). Sori are arranged between midvein and margin (middle). Previous year's green blades persist flat to ground (bottom left).

Marginal Wood Fern *Dryopteris marginalis*

Rocky wooded slopes and in ravines among roots and rocks.

Nature Notes:

As with the Evergreen Wood Fern, old fronds persist through the winter and provide important energy and nutrition in the spring.

Many species of *Dryopteris* and *Polystichum* have adaptations to lie protected under the snow. Adequate snow cover protects the fronds from frost damage. Climate change may reduce the snowpack in some regions leading to frost damage and lower growth rate in those species. Marginal Wood Fern's leathery fronds may provide an additional benefit to this species in low snow years.

Large leathery, evergreen grayish fern growing in scattered clumps with dead fronds persisting at the base.

Description: *Fronds* 12-39 inches long; 4-10 inches wide. *Pinnae* are lance-shaped, widest at base, rapidly tapering to a point at tip. *Rachis* looks pale and chaffy underneath with small scales. Look for a stout, shaggy *rhizome* with large golden-brown scales. As the name implies, the *sori* are arranged near the margins ↑, appear prominent and in well-spaced rows; dark brown when mature.

Similar Species: This species is easily identified by the untoothed margin ↑ of pinnae lobes, marginal sori and evergreen habit.

forests

Sori are arranged near the margins of the pinnules; also note the untoothed margins (top).

forests

Common Oak Fern   *Gymnocarpium dryopteris*

Moist, shaded, rocky soil in cool, coniferous and mixed woods.

Nature Notes:

Gymnocarpium is Greek for "naked fruit," which refers to the lack of an indusium covering the spores.

Common Oak Fern is clearly the most common, but keep your eyes open for the differences—you might come across the other rarely seen species. On occasion we learn that "rare" is misapplied to plant and animal species and only remains because not enough people know what to look for. Which of these three species do you see?

Smaller, delicate, bright green three-parted fern tilted mostly parallel to the ground.

Description: *Fronds* 5-18 inches long. New fronds emerge most all summer. *Blade* is 3-parted with distinct stalks ↑ and each is deeply divided. *Pinnules* of lowest pinnae cut almost to midvein. The upper surface lacks glandular hairs; lower surface with few or no glandular hairs. *Rachis* is green, delicate. *Stipe* extends to 4-11 inches long and longer than blade. *Sori* are small, round, few, near margin. *Basal pinnae* nearly equal to the whole upper portion of the blade.

Similar Species: Nahanni Oak Fern (*Gymnocarpium jessoense*) is rare in our area; grows on cool rocky crevices and talus slopes. Lacks glandular hairs on upper surface of blade only and the two basal pinnae are curved toward the tip of the blade. Limestone Oak Fern (*G. robertianum*) is also a rare fern of cool, calcareous forests. Lower two triangular pinnae are noticeably smaller than the middle pinnae. The entire fern is densely glandular and aromatic.

forests

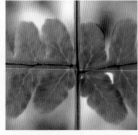

Limestone Oak Fern
Gymnocarpium robertianum

Nahanni
Oak Fern
Gymnocarpium jessoense

Limestone Oak Fern
Gymnocarpium robertianum

Nahanni Oak Fern
Gymnocarpium jessoense

Common Oak Fern is a distinctly three-parted fern; all blades are roughly equal in size (main photo opposite page). Nahanni Oak Fern's basal pinnae are smaller than the main blade and curved toward the tip (middle left). Limestone Oak Fern is entirely densely glandular and aromatic.

forests

Common Oak Fern
Gymnocarpium dryopteris

Limestone Oak Fern
Gymnocarpium robertianum

Nahanni Oak Fern
Gymnocarpium jessoense

Northern Beech Fern *Phegopteris connectilis*

Wet, rocky areas near running water or in shaded, rich, moist forests and occasionally in rock crevices.

Nature Notes:

Current logging practices encourage the harvest of all wood products. This results in the reduction of dead wood (coarse woody debris) on the forest floor. Though presence of dead wood clearly benefits lichens and mosses, other organisms (including Beech Ferns) also benefit from the presence of this coarse woody debris. Decaying stems and logs provide diverse habitat niches and a variety of soil nutrients and organic matter. Should we harvest fewer acres more intensively or cut more and leave coarse materials behind? Not an easy choice.

Common, light green ankle-high triangular fern.

Description: Very common light green fern with narrow triangular fronds. *Connectilis* refers to the fact that the upper *pinnae* are fused toward the frond tip. *Fronds* 6-14 inches long; 4-8 inches wide; tilted backward and cut into 12 pairs of opposite *pinnae*. *Rachis* green, scaly, hairy ↑ above and beneath; not winged at lowest *pinnae* (which is also shorter than pinnae above and reflexed or drooping ↑). *Stip* 6-14 inches long and straw colored (usually about 1/3 longer than blade). *Sori* are small, round and near margins at ends of veins. No *indusium*.

Similar Species: Broad Beech Fern (*Phegopteris hexagonoptera*) is strictly terrestrial. The lower pinnae are longest and have hexagonal wings ↑ at the segment base.

forests

Broad Beech Fern
Phegopteris hexagonoptera

Broad Beech Fern
Phegopteris hexagonoptera

Lowest pinnae distinctly paired and pulled outward from main frond (reflexed) (top left). Rachis green above, hairy and stipe straw colored. Broad Beech Fern differs in having a distinctly winged rachis (bottom left) and its lower pinnae are longest.

Northern Beech Fern
Phegopteris connectilis

Broad Beech Fern
Phegopteris hexagonoptera

forests

Ostrich Fern *Matteuccia struthiopteris*

Rich woods along stream banks or in places with damp soils.

Nature Notes:

Sterile fronds wither with first frost. Fertile fronds persist through the winter as stiff, dark brown structures.

Fertile fronds release green spores early in spring when the winds can disperse them more easily.

Fiddleheads are edible and harvested for commercial use especially in rural northeastern North America. These are essentially the only edible fiddleheads in our area. You might simply boil them in salted water and serve like asparagus with a little browned butter drizzled over the top.

Larger ostrich-feather shaped fern forms distinct vase-like clumps; often in large colonies.

Description: Tall, erect arching fern growing in distinct tufts. Each *blade* is a rich green ostrich-feather shape ↑ to 50 inches long and 5-10 inches wide; cut into 20-60 pairs of pinnae that are deeply cut into long, alternate lobes. Lower *pinnae* much smaller and sometimes clasping the rachis. *Rachis* green, stout with whitish hairs. *Stipe* much shorter than blade, deeply grooved ↑ at base with rounded back. *Fertile frond* separate and distinctive ↑; to 28 inches. *Rhizome* with emerging symmetrical crown; spreads by many underground runners.

Similar Species: It might be confused with Sensitive Fern (pg. 108) during winter; look for distinct groove in the rachis of Ostrich Fern. In summer, sterile fronds can be confused with Interrupted (pg. 86) and Cinnamon (pg. 110) Ferns; look for the ostrich-feather shape and very short pinnae at the base of the rachis.

wet areas

This species gets its odd common name from the resemblance of its blade to the shape of an ostrich feather (main photo opposite page). Fertile fronds distinct from sterile fronds (top left). Ostrich Ferns often form large waist-high colonies. Fertile fronds persist through winter (middle right). Stipe is distinctly grooved (bottom right).

Minn.

Wisc.

Mich.

wet areas

Bead Fern (Sensitive Fern)   *Onoclea sensibilis*

Open swamps, wet areas, marshes and low woods.

Nature Notes:

The common name Sensitive Fern is supposedly in reference to its sensitivity to fall frosts. However, the Latin *sensibilis* does not mean "sensitive;" instead, it means "of the senses." In fact, this fern is not very sensitive and there are other species obviously more sensitive. It might be more sensible to use the older common name of Bead Fern in reference to the fertile stems that look much like a string of beads (and persist into winter). Are there other species you feel have misleading common names? What common names do you prefer?

Simple-cut triangular fern forming dense colonies.

Description: Sterile triangular frond 8-40 inches tall is very light green and cut into approximately 12 pairs of opposite simple pinnae ↑. *Fertile frond* 10-12 inches tall narrow with small, hard, beadlike ↑ divisions which is at first green turning dark brown at maturity. *Rachis* of sterile frond smooth, winged, glistening. *Stipe* usually longer than blade. *Rhizome* is stout, forking near the surface. *Fiddleheads* are a pale red.

Similar Species: None. Very distinctive. Related and some vague similiarities to Ostrich Fern (pg. 106), but all you need do to confirm this species is to look at the stipe and rachis—Sensitive Fern is round to oval; Ostrich Fern has a deep groove.

These ferns form dense colonies (top). Fertile fronds with small, beadlike divisions give rise to its common name—Bead Fern (bottom right). Fertile fronds stand out in winter (below).

wet areas

Cinnamon Fern   *Osmunda cinnamomea*

Swamps, bog margins and wooded stream banks in fairly acid soils.

Nature Notes:

The name *Osmunda* may have come from Saxon mythology. The Saxon god Osmunder (aka, Thor from Norse mythology) hid his family inside a large group of ferns to protect them from danger.

The fern forms huge colonies with densely matted root-stocks. These root fibers are often harvested and used in the propagation of orchids.

"Cinnamon" in the name refers to the color (not the taste) of the fertile fronds. In early Fall, while wandering among wetlands, look for the brilliant rusty-orange fronds standing out among mosses and early fall foliage (photo on opposite page).

A large, clump-forming fern with short-lived wand-like cinnamon-colored fertile fronds.

Description: Large, clump-forming fern with arching fronds and distinct cinnamon-colored *fertile fronds* ↑ lasting for a few weeks. *Fronds* are 20-60 inches long and mostly erect with a pinkish stipe. *Fertile fronds* wither and remain draped around the frond bases ↑. *Spores* are green and short-lived. Pale tufts of wool are at the base of each *pinnae* ↑. *Rachis* is smooth, green with pale wool on early season growth. Slender, oblong *pinnae* are cut deeply into lobes.

Similar Species: Interrupted Fern (pg. 86) can be mistaken, especially when spore-bearing structures are not obvious. Look for pale tufts of wool at the base of each pinnae and search hard for the withered fertile fronds lying at the base of the clump of fronds to confirm that you have Cinnamon Fern. You might also notice wet ground below you.

wet areas

Clumps turn brilliant rusty orange in fall. The cinnamon-colored fertile fronds last for a few weeks (bottom left and middle). Withered fertile fronds can be seen laying prostrate amidst new growth (below). Pale tufts of wool are found at the base of each pinna (bottom right).

Minn.

Wisc.

Mich.

wet areas

Royal Fern *Osmunda regalis*

Swamps, low woods, wet meadows and along stream banks.

Nature Notes:

The name Royal Fern is said to have come from the fact that it is among the largest and most imposing ferns in our area.

Also called "locust fern" due to its vague resemblance to the leaf arrangement of a locust tree.

When in water, it will reach heights over 6 feet.

Regal indeed, this fern is also known as Flowering Fern because of the reddish spore masses that, from a distance, look like flowers.

This species can be found in Africa, South America, Europe, Asia and North America—that is remarkable for any species!

A very large fern that looks much like a locust tree with rusty red spore-bearing tufts overtopping the entire plant.

Description: This is a very large fern (3 or more feet tall) whose blades look like the leaves of a locust tree. *Pinnules* are pale green and oblong, resembling locust leaves ↑. The fertile portions are perched at the top of the fronds ↑. They are rusty red ↑ turning to brown as the season continues.

Similar Species: The leaf structure looks much like a form of honey locust, a tree of dry woodlands. Otherwise, you will never mistake this fern for any other species in our range.

Fronds cut like leaves of locust tree (top left). Eye-catching rusty red spore-bearing tufts are obvious even from a distance (top right). Paddling along shorelines is a good way to find dense colonies of Royal Ferns.

Minn.

Wisc.

Mich.

wet areas

Goldie's Wood Fern   *Dryopteris goldiana*

Rich soils of cool, moist woods; especially in ravines and on swamp edges.

Nature Notes:

Named after John Goldie (a Scottish naturalist) who came to America in 1817 hoping to work on the Lewis and Clark materials and explore the North American interior. That didn't pan out, so he walked from Montreal through Albany, New York and on to New Jersey. By 1819 he "commenced my long talked of journey" among the eastern Great Lakes. Self-financed and on foot, he made many collections including the root of what we now call Goldie's Wood Fern. How far would you walk to explore and discover?

Larger, bright green arching fern with an abruptly tapered frond growing in clusters.

Description: The largest of our wood ferns. *Fronds* are 1-4 feet long; 6-16 inches wide. *Blade* is mostly oval with parallel sides and abruptly pointed tip ↑. *Pinnules* are in 18 pairs, mostly opposite with rounded forward pointed tips and margins slightly toothed at ends of veins. The green *rachis* has pale scales ↑. *Stipe* brownish.

Similar Species: A southern Michigan species, Clinton's Wood Fern (*Dryopteris clintoniana*), is a hybrid of Goldie's Wood Fern and Crested Wood Fern (pg. 116) and so there are intermediate qualities.

wet areas

Lowermost pinnae are the longest overall (top). Blade tip is abruptly pointed. Rachis has pale scales (bottom right). Clinton's Wood Fern (*Dryopteris clintoniana*) has intermediate qualities of Goldie's Wood Fern and Crested Wood Fern.

Clinton's Wood Fern
Dryopteris clintoniana

wet areas

Crested Wood Fern *Dryopteris cristata*

Wet, swampy woods and open wetlands, alder thickets
and mossy fens/bogs.

Nature Notes:

Genetic diversity in a
species or population
may adversely affect the
potential of that species to
cope with environmental
challenges including climate
change. *Dryopteris cristata*
is just one species with low
genetic diversity. Though we
can't change the pace of
evolution (and potential of
genetic diversity in species),
this knowledge can be used
to make predictions of how
species diversity and eco-
systems may change as our
climates continue to shift.

Root extracts from this fern
have been used to expel
intestinal parasites.

Shiny, bright green mid-sized fern with hori-
zontally-oriented pinnae.

Description: Erect fronds (1-2 feet long;
3-5 inches wide) with widely spaced *pinnae*
oriented horizontally ↑. *Fertile fronds* are tall
and narrow. *Sterile fronds* usually shorter,
spreading and evergreen. *Blade* narrows with
sides becoming almost parallel. *Basal pinnae* obviously triangular and blunt ↑. *Rachis*
green, stout, scaly on lower parts ↑; stipe 10
inches long. Creeping *rhizome* is dark brown
and stout. *Sori* are prominent halfway between
midvein and margin.

Similar Species: Crested Wood Fern
hybridizes with five species. All of the hybrids
can be identified by overall narrow blades and
the triangular basal pinnae.

Rachis green, stout and scaly on lower parts (top left). Pinnae are horizontally oriented. Sori prominent between midvein and margin (bottom left). Basal pinnae are triangular and blunt (bottom right).

Minn.

Wisc.

Mich.

wet areas

Northern Marsh Fern *Thelypteris palustris*

Moist, sunny areas of swamps, marshes and shorelines.

Nature Notes:

Grows best in low pH, wet systems.

Rarely will you find it in standing water, but it does grow on floating moss mats on the edge of cool, clear lakes.

Marsh Fern Moth (*Fagitana littera*) caterpillars feed on this fern and it is the only host plant for this rare moth.

The most immediate threat to this fern and moth species is habitat loss to purple loosestrife and other shoreline damage.

Smaller to mid-sized delicate fern growing singly.

Description: *Fronds* 7-36 inches long; 2-8 inches wide. Cut into 12 pairs of opposite *pinnae* that are lance-shaped and cut nearly to midvein (veins are forked). Margins rounded or blunt-tipped lobes ↑. *Fertile pinnules* have a revolute margin. *Rachis* green, smooth ↑. *Stipe* 5-28 inches long; longer than blade; smooth, green above and brown to black at base. *Rhizome* slender, black and widely creeping. *Sori* numerous, round, mostly on upper pinnae in close rows near the midvein. *Indusium* pale, narrow, often hairy.

Similar Species: Lady Fern (pg. 88) can be confused, but grows in clumps and has toothed margins.

Delicate fern of mossy shorelines (top right). Pinnae are cut nearly to the midvein (top right) and rounded at tips (bottom left). Stipe is green above and brown to black at base (bottom left). Rachis is smooth (bottom right).

Minn.

Wisc.

Mich.

wet areas

Braun's Holly Fern *Polystichum braunii*

Moist, cool, deep forests along primary rivulets in the watershed.

Nature Notes:

Some ferns thrive in a wide range of habitats. Others, like Braun's Holly Fern, can be quite limited. Your best bet to find this species? Explore the initial trickles of streams—those tiny rivulets that only run during rainstorms.

Polystichum is Greek for "many rows" in reference to sorus pattern.

Tight fiddleheads are established in later summer and are somewhat visible deep in the center of the cluster in Fall and Winter.

Named in honor of Alexander Braun—a pioneer in the 1830s of the study of phyllotaxy. Phyllotactic spirals (derived mathematically from Fibonacci ratios) describe the distinct patterns of leaves on stems.

Relatively uncommon mid-sized, dark green, densely scaly fern.

Description: Large, dark green fronds with dense, reddish brown scales on *stipe* and *rachis*. *Fronds* form a dense cluster from the central rhizome. Fronds 1-3 feet tall. *Blades* thick, arching, widest above the middle and tapering at both ends. Semi-evergreen. *Pinnules* often overlapping ↑; margins with bristly teeth ↑. *Rachis* very scaly ↑. *Stipe* short covered with brown scales. *Rhizome* scaly, stout and brown. *Sori* small and round in two rows near midvein.

Similar Species: Northern Holly Fern (*Polystichum lonchitis*) is a very rare mid-sized, dark green, narrow ↑ leathery and scaly fern of north facing ledges moist talus. Margins of pinnae have small spines. Stipe blackish. Blade is widest above the middle. Sori crowded to upper half of the blade. Pinnae with upward pointing lobes.

Northern Holly Fern
Polystichum lonchitis

Northern Holly Fern
Polystichum lonchitis

Northern Holly Fern
Polystichum lonchitis

Braun's pinnules are overlapping (middle right); with bristly margins (middle right). Rachis with dense reddish-brown scales (top). Blades taper at both ends. Holly Fern (*Polystichum lonchitis*) has long and narrow blades (bottom right).

Braun's
Holly Fern
Polystichum braunii

Northern
Holly Fern
Polystichum lonchitis

wet areas

FERNS OF WET AREAS

Rock Polypody *Polypodium virginianum*

Moss-covered boulders and ledges and semi-shaded rocky surfaces or stumps.

Nature Notes:

Also called Rock-cap Fern.

Polypodium from Greek for "many feet" in reference to rootstock.

The rhizome has a slight licorice taste.

Sunflecks (short bursts of intense sunlight) can be a major source of energy for understory plants such as Rock Polypody. Sunflecks can also damage delicate tissues. Thriving in the dark understory requires various adaptations for increasing the photosynthetic potential while also protecting plants from the damaging sunrays. Rock Polypody is obviously successful here. It is also one of the few plants to remain green year-round.

Small, leathery, evergreen simple-cut fern forming dense communities on cliffs, boulders

Description: *Fronds* can grow 16 inches, but commonly smaller. *Blade* is leathery, deep green on both sides; 3 inches wide near the middle. Cut almost completely to rachis into pairs of smooth, alternate blunt rounded lobes ↑. *Rachis* is smooth, green. *Stipe* up to ¹/₃ length of blade and swollen at base where it attaches to the rhizome. *Rhizome* spreads and creeps producing rows of fronds and can be exposed at the surface. *Sori* large, round ↑, pale brown in rows on either side of midvein; releasing spores in fall, but obvious all year round. *Sori* with *indusium*.

Similar Species: Considering the location and growth form, you won't mistake this fern with any other fern in our area. Head to the extreme west coast or Appalachians for other species in this genus.

...arge sori are in rows (top) and release their spores in fall. Rock Polypody forms dense ...ommunities, especially on moss-covered boulders. Green fronds persist through winter.

Minn.

Wisc.

Mich.

rocky areas

Smooth Cliff Brake   *Pellaea glabella*

Cliff faces often associated with, but not limited to, lakeshores.

Nature Notes:

Cliff communities may serve this (and other) species well. Most people look at rugged cliff faces as inhospitable places with little vegetation. As a result, they may be one of the few landscapes left untouched and serving as refuges for biodiversity worthy of our protection.

Presence of Cliff Brake may indicate an old growth system no less significant or noteworthy than the more obvious old growth cedar, pine or maple forests capturing our attention.

Tufted fern with gray-green oval leaflets connected to dark wiry stems.

Description: Tufts of stiff, wiry, bluish gray-green fronds with smooth reddish-brown stipes. They grow from shady cliff edges and rock slopes in dry vertical or overhanging cliffs. *Fronds* are 4-16 inches long and 1-3 inches wide. Clustered fronds; sterile and fertile fronds similar in shape; sterile fronds are shorter and less divided. *Blade* cut into 5-10 opposite *pinnae*. *Rachis* is brown throughout and smooth (hairless and shiny) ↑. *Sori* beneath are hidden by in-rolled margins of pinnae ↑ or pinnules.

Similar Species: Purple Stem Cliff Brake (*Pellaea atropurpurea*) is very similar, but has obvious hairs on the rachis ↑.

Oval leaflets on brown wiry rachis (top left). Sori of Smooth Cliff Brake hidden by in-rolled margins (top left). Purple Stem Cliff Brake (*Pellaea atropurpurea*) has obvious hairs on a purple rachis (below).

Purple Stem Cliff Brake
Pellaea atropurpurea

Minn.

Wisc.

Mich.

Smooth
Cliff Brake
Pellaea glabella

Minn.

Wisc.

Mich.

Purple Stem
Cliff Brake
Pellaea atropurpurea

rocky areas

Slender Cliff Brake   *Cryptogramma stelleri*

Shaded, moist cliff cracks and ledges.

Nature Notes:

Also called Steller's Rock Brake, this fern is named in honor of German naturalist George Wilhelm Steller (also know for Stellers Jay, Stellers Sea Lion, etc). A naturalist, physician and explorer, Steller is considered a primary pioneer of Alaskan natural history—exploring there in the 1740s.

Cryptogramma means "hidden rows of sori." Pry back the inrolled margins of the fern to look for the spore structures.

Fragile, small, parsley-like fern.

Description: Fragile, small fern found on shaded, moist cliff crevices and rock ledges. Sterile and fertile fronds differ in size and shape. *Fronds* 3-8 inches long. *Blade* triangular, widest near the base. Smooth and fragile. *Fertile pinnae* narrower and *sterile pinnae* with broad, round outlines. *Fertile blade* a third larger with segments entire. *Rachis* smooth and green ↑. *Stipe* longer than blade and darker below with pale green above. *Sori* in inrolled margins of fertile pinnae ↑.

Similar Species: Similar in appearance to smaller blades of Smooth Cliff Brake (pg. 124). Look at the distinctly green rachis of Slender Cliff Brake.

Fertile pinnae are narrow with inrolled margins (top); sterile pinnae are broad and rounded; resembling parsley (bottom left). Rachis is green.

Minn.

Wisc.

Mich.

Walking Fern   *Asplenium rhizophyllum*

Shaded, moss-covered boulders and outcrops.

Nature Notes:

Sometimes growing on the ground or moss covered logs, when the tip touches the ground it can root and sprout a new plant (hence the name "walking" fern).

This fern can be found along the Niagara Escarpment or other alkaline rock substrates.

Conservation of this species will require that we maintain an overstory of old growth—best if it is an overstory of old growth—of broad-leaved trees providing adequate shade to maintain cool temperatures and high moisture levels. Intact old systems are rare and so are these ferns.

A rare and very distinct fern with long, narrow, pointed, simple leaves.

Description: This is a very rare fern especially in our area. *Fronds* are 1-15 inches long and 1-2 inches wide at the base. *Blades* are evergreen and slightly leathery. The base is somewhat heart-shaped tapering to a long point ↑. *Stipe* is slender, flattened and grooved above with a dark brown base. *Sori* are often numerous and scattered throughout the blade at the vein junctions.

Similar Species: Hart's-Tongue Fern (*Asplenium scolopendrium*) is another very rare, simple leaved fern with a more heart-shaped base and a blunt tip ↑. *Sori* in linear rows ↑.

rocky areas

Hart's-Tongue Fern
Asplenium scolopendrium

Hart's-Tongue Fern
Asplenium scolopendrium

Frond tips root and grow new fronds allowing them to "walk" across the landscape (top). Hart's-Tongue Fern (*Asplenium scolopendrium*) is another very rare find. Its blades have a more heart-shaped base and a blunt tip. Also note the sori in linear rows (bottom right).

Walking Fern
Asplenium rhizophyllum

Hart's-Tongue Fern
Asplenium scolopendrium

rocky areas

Maidenhair Spleenwort *Asplenium trichomanes*

Cliff-dwelling fern of moist crevices and ledges.

Nature Notes:

Asplenium refers to the supposed cure of diseases of the spleen. *Trichomanes* means a tangled mass of hair.

If you want to find this species, search for the largest cliffs in our range and then focus your time on the most prominent cliff features in that spot. It won't be easy, but that's precisely where this species thrives. You will likely only see it if you enjoy rock climbing on the most difficult routes. Remember good climbing ethics and avoid damaging this rare species.

Rare, tiny, wiry fronds growing in clumps.

Description: Narrow *fronds* are approximately 2-10 inches long with a tapering pattern toward both the top and bottom of the frond. Dark green with about 20 pairs of *pinnae*. *Fertile fronds* are upright and sterile fronds usually flat to the surface. *Pinnae* are about a quarter inch long; smaller toward both ends of the blade. *Lower pinnae* more widely spaced; upper pinnae often crowded and overlapping. *Rachis* wiry; dark purple to brown ↑. *Stipe* is 1/3 as long as blade. *Sori* 2-4 pairs per *pinnae*.

Similar Species: Green Spleenwort (*Asplenium viride*) is a very rare, small fern with rounded pinnae. Rachis is green ↑ and delicate. Will sometimes grow alongside this species.

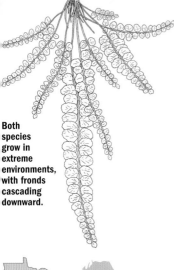

Both species grow in extreme environments, with fronds cascading downward.

Tiny, distinct pinnae paired on a wiry, dark rachis (top). Green Spleenwort (*Asplenium viride*) has very small rounded pinnae on green rachis (below).

Green Spleenwort
Asplenium viride

Maidenhair Spleenwort
Asplenium trichomanes

Green Spleenwort
Asplenium viride

rocky areas

Fragrant Fern *Dryopteris fragrans*

Cool, shaded, north-facing cliffs and talus slopes.

Nature Notes:

Look for the old clumps usually persisting for 2-3 years. You can see that the green fronds turn brown and then gray.

Among botanists of the early 1900s, field notes often imply that presence of this species was a highlight for them. While other species were simply listed, words like "glorious" and "finally" accompanied notes when botanists of the south found these species on their forays north. What species bring you joy when you see them?

Dark green fronds with gray-brown clumps of old, persisting fronds at the base ↑.

Description: *Fronds* are 3-16 inches long. *Blades* are the same width most of blade length, leathery in texture and covered with glands ↑ on upper and lower surface that give off a sweet, fruity fragrance. *Pinnae* about one inch long with margins often rolled under. Margins with rounded teeth and no bristles. *Rachis* glandular. *Stipe* very short covered with brown scales and surrounded by withered fronds of previous years. *Sori* large, crowded, chocolate-brown, cover most of lower surface. *Indusia* kidney-shaped, large, scale-like.

Similar Species: Rusty Cliff Fern (pg. 140) looks similar at first glance. Look for the persistent withered fronds draping at the base to confirm Fragrant Fern.

rocky areas

Blades are same width as most of the length. Short stipe covered with brown scales (bottom right). Clumps of old fronds persist 2-3 years (top right); brown may be 2 years old and gray might be 3 years old. Obvious on rock faces through winter. Stipe has abundant brown scales (bottom right).

Minn.

Wisc.

Mich.

Bulblet Bladder Fern *Cystopteris bulbifera*

Damp, shady talus slopes and cliff edges.

Nature Notes:

There are 2-12 bulblets per frond. Bulblets drop off and germinate into new plants increasing the overall reproductive success.

When you find one individual, you will likely see others growing in a green cascade flowing down a jumble of moss-covered, damp rocks. Watch your step to avoid a tumble and to avoid damaging this delicate, graceful fern. Even better, leave no trace and observe from a distance.

Long-tapering, delicate, mid-sized graceful fern.

Description: *Frond* is lax, long, triangular ↑. *Fronds* are 1-3 feet long and approximately 3 inches wide—very narrow and long. Pale green to yellow-green *pinnae* perpendicular to rachis drooping at the end. Small, pea-like *bulblets* on underside of blade ↑. *Rachis* shining yellow and covered with gland-tipped hairs. *Stipe* (much shorter than rachis) reddish to pink ↑ when young and turning straw-colored, green later. *Sori* between margin and midvein or pinnule.

Similar Species: Laurentian Bladder Fern (*Cystopteris laurentiana*) is a fertile hybrid derived from this species and Fragile Fern (page 136). Very similar to Fragile Fern, but it has sparse gland-tipped hairs and sometimes a few bulblets that are small, reddish, scaly and misshapen.

rocky areas

Laurentian Bladder Fern
Cystopteris laurentiana

Fragile Fern
Cystopteris fragilis

Small, pea-like bulblets are found on the underside of the blade (top left, right). Frond is long and triangular (middle right). Stipe reddish (middle left).

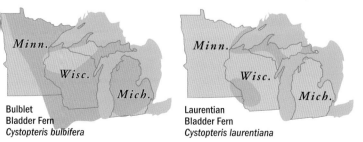

Bulblet
Bladder Fern
Cystopteris bulbifera

Laurentian
Bladder Fern
Cystopteris laurentiana

FERNS OF ROCKY AREAS

Fragile Fern *Cystoperis fragilis*

Shaded cliffs and rocky crevices.

Nature Notes:

Fragile Fern is most definitely a delicate species growing in a harsh, unforgiving environment.

Rock climbers of long ago would routinely "clean" routes by scraping mosses, lichens and ferns from rock faces. Today, climbing ethics are improved and it is considered a badge of honor to climb a face cleanly by not "cleaning" the route. Climbing in harmony with the delicate, fragile wonders of a unique habitat is good for our environment too!

Small, very delicate, bright green fern in clusters.

Description: *Fronds* 4-10 inches long; 1-3 inches wide. *Blade* lanceolate with pointed tips, widest just below middle. *Pinnae* (usually 12 pairs) at right angles to rachis. *Lower pinnae* widely separated. *Rachis* smooth. *Stipe* shorter than blade, brittle, deep reddish-brown at very base becoming green above. Some withered fronds will remain from previous year ↑. *Sori* few and scattered on veins (roundish and covered by an *indusium* that is hood-like) ↑. No bulblets and no glandular hairs on rachis.

Similar Species: Mackay's Brittle Fern (*Cystopteris tenuis*) forms small clumps of bright green fronds growing on shaded cliff faces and forest floors. Pinnae are typically arching toward the tip of the frond compared to pinnae at right angles to rachis in Fragile Fern. If teeth are present, they will tend to be more rounded in *C. tenuis* and more pointed in Fragile Fern.

Mackay's Brittle Fern
Cystopteris tenuis

Sori roundish and scattered on veins (top). Rachis smooth and green (top); stipe reddish-brown below. A few withered fronds remain from the previous year (main photo opposite page).

Fragile Fern
Cystopteris fragilis

Mackay's
Brittle Fern
Cystopteris tenuis

rocky areas

Smooth Cliff Fern *Woodsia glabella*

Moist, shaded rock crevices.

Nature Notes:

This genus of ferns was named in honor of Joseph Woods. Born in England in 1776, Joseph Woods was a Quaker architect, botanist and geologist. In his late 50s, Woods' interest in architecture waned and his passion with botany took over. At the age of 74 he published *The Tourist's Flora,* drawing on his many field excursions in Europe. What book will you write at that age?

Tiny, rare fern in erect, dense tufts.

Description: Delicate, pale green, smooth *blade* with old, broken *stipes* in persistent clusters of nearly equal height at the base. *Fronds* 1-6 inches long; about ¼-½ inch wide. *Rachis* is smooth, green. Yellowish-green *stipe* is shorter than blade, smooth above the joint at middle; brown scales below the joint. *Sori* small, distinct, near margins ↑. *Indusium* a tiny disk with short, hairlike projections.

Similar Species: Alpine Cliff Fern (*Woodsia alpina*) is a very small, rare fern of cool rocky crevices. Old, broken stipes form persistent clusters of nearly equal length at the base of fronds. Fronds are very similar, except that *Woodsia alpina* has scattered hairs and scales ↑. Blades narrow, slightly narrower at base and usually blunt tipped. Stipe short, reddish brown to purple at base with a swollen joint below the middle; slightly scaly.

Indusium tissue, covering sori

Alpine Cliff Fern
Woodsia alpina

Alpine Cliff Fern
Woodsia alpina

Yellowish-green stipe is jointed and has brown scales below the joint. Indusia are tiny, umbrella-like disks with short hairlike projections which cover the sori (found near margins). Old stipes form persistent clusters of nearly equal lengths. Alpine Cliff Fern (*Woodsia alpina*) has a reddish-brown to purple stipe (bottom right).

Smooth
Cliff Fern
Woodsia glabella

Alpine
Cliff Fern
Woodsia alpina

rocky areas

Rusty Cliff Fern   *Woodsia ilvensis*

Somewhat common in full sun on rocky outcrops.

Nature Notes:

You will notice that the whole plant turns rusty brown during dry periods and sends up new green fronds when rains return.

Also known as Rusty Woodsia.

Estonia (south of Finland) served as a site for an attempted re-introduction of Rusty Cliff Fern in 1997—twenty years after it was last located there in the wild. Results ten years later were mixed. The difficulty of planting in microhabitats of bare rock and crevices limited the success of re-introduction. Consider the growing conditions. Can you imagine planting and keeping tiny ferns alive on bare rock?

Small, densely hairy fern forms distinct ankle-high tufts turning rusty with age.

Description: *Fronds* 2-10 inches long; about 1 inch wide. *Blade* stiff, erect with pointed tips. *Fronds* deep green above with silvery white undersides turning rusty brown in fall ↑ and during dry seasons. The oval *pinnae* are stemless and slightly pointed. The straw-colored to green *rachis* has abundant hairs and scales. Shiny brown *stipe* is jointed about 1 inch above rhizome; the bristly stubble persists at a uniform height ↑ for many years. *Sori* are small, near margin and hidden by scales and hairs.

Similar Species: Not only is this our most common *Woodsia*, the dense hairs and jointed stipe will isolate this species from the other related species. Look for both characteristics.

rocky areas

The rachis is densely hairy. Stipes are jointed, and the stubble persists in uniform height (bottom right). The "rusty" in its common name refers to the golden brown the fern turns in fall.

Minn.

Wisc.

Mich.

Oregon Cliff Fern   *Woodsia oregona*

Cliffs, crevices and talus.

Nature Notes:

Because the stipes of these species are not jointed, you should poke around where they emerge at the substrate to look for remains of previous years. The "stubble" will be uneven. Also, look for distinctly multi-lobed indusia and veins that do not reach the leaf margin. Both are diagnostic features for all *Woodsia* species.

Uncommon, small clumped fern.

Description: This western species has reddish brown nonjointed *stipes*. *Frond* lacks hairs and scales, but the *blade* is glandular. Look for long, thread-like tips on *indusial segments*.

Similar Species: Mountain Cliff Fern (*Woodsia scopulina*) has distinctly toothed pinna margins with many flat whitish hairs. Blade is glandular. Stipe not jointed and relatively brittle.

Stipes are reddish brown and nonjointed. Blades are glandular. Mountain Cliff Fern (*Woodsia scopulina*) has distinctly toothed pinna margins.

Mountain Cliff Fern *Woodsia scopulina*

Oregon Cliff Fern
Woodsia oregona

Mountain Cliff Fern
Woodsia scopulina

rocky areas

Glossary

Acroscopic: the edge of a pinna, for example, growing toward the apex or tip of the frond.

Acute: tapering toward a tip with both sides straight, not curved.

Alternate: a stem or leaf, for example, inserted at a single point along some axis without the same occurring on the opposite side of the axis.

Angiosperm: a plant bearing flowers and producing seeds in an ovary

Annual constriction: a narrowed portion of the stem of clubmosses, for example, created by the end of one growing season and start of another.

Annulus: a row of thick and thin-walled cells of the spore case that functions to open and release spores in ferns.

Antheridium: the male sex organ borne on the underside of the gametophyte that produces sperm.

Appressed: close to the surface and not spreading.

Archegonium: the female sex organ borne on the underside of the gametophyte that produces eggs.

Auricle: a low, basal lobe of a leaf structure.

Axil: the point between a stalk and anything (petiole, rachis, midrib, for example) arising from it.

Basiscopic: the edge of a pinna, for example, growing toward the base of the frond.

Bipinnate: twice pinnate; with a midrib of one pinna arising from the midrib of another, larger pinna.

Blade: the thin, broad par of a leaf or frond.

Bog: a wet, acidic, nutrient-poor peatland characterized by sphagnum mosses, shrubs and sedges that receive nutrients only from precipitation

Boreal: far northern latitudes.

Bulblet: a small pea-like structure borne on a stem or leaf serving to vegetatively reproduce the fern.

Calcareous: containing calcium carbonate, or calcite, chalk, with a pH greater than 7.

Chlorophyll: green pigments coloring the plant and serving to absorb the sun's radiant energy in photosynthesis.

Cilia: short hairs typically along a margin of a leaf or pinna.

Circumboreal: refers to species distribution that circles the earth's boreal regions.

Circumpolar: living or found in the vicinity of a terrestrial pole.

Clone: an organism produced asexually from and is genetically identical to a single ancestor.

Compound: referring to a leaf having two or more leaflets.

Cone: a tight cluster of modified, spore-bearing leaves found at the branch tips.

Cordate: heart-shaped.

Corm: a solid, globular rootstock found in *Isoetes*.

Costa: the midrib of a simple frond, pinna or pinnule.

Creeping: growing horizontally in or on the soil.

Cristate: having crests or tasseled margins.

Crozier: a young coiled fern frond or fiddlehead.

Cut: in reference to a dissection or division of a pinna, for example.

Deciduous: detaching or shed annually and not evergreen.

Dichotomous: regularly forked into pairs.

Diploid: having two sets of chromosomes.

Disjunct: a population of organisms separated geographically and growing outside the main range of that species.

Elaters: strap-shaped appendages of the spores of *Equisetum*.

Entire: having a smooth, unmodified margin.

Eusporangiate: ferns (including *Ophioglossum* and *Botrychium*) with thick-walled sporangium containing many spores.

Evergreen: remaining green throughout the winter, but may brown and wither during the following growing season.

False indusium: an indusium formed by a rolled margin of the leaf of Adiantum and Pellaea, for example.

Fern allies: those groups of plants that reproduce by spores and have a life cycle similar to true ferns, but differ in how they bear spores and by leaf structure; Fern allies include horsetails, clubmosses, quillworts and spikemosses.

Fertile: usually referring to fern leaves that bear sori.

Fiddlehead: a young fern leaf or bud that is coiled in a spiral pattern and also called a crozier.

Flora: a list of species found in a particular geographical region.

Form: a minor variant of a species.

Frond: the leaf of a fern consisting of a petiole and blade.

Gametophyte: a small plant growing directly from spores and bearing the sex organs that produce gametes.

Gemmae: small, readily detached vegetative structures that can grow into new plants found on some *Huperzia*, for example.

Genus: a group of related species.

Gland: a structure found on the surface of a plant that secretes a waxy or resinous substance.

Gymnosperm: a group of plants (pines and spruces, for example) with ovules that are not enclosed in an ovary.

Habitat: where a plant lives.

Haploid: having one set of chromosomes.

Herbaceous: typically applied to a frond that dies back to the ground at the end of a growing season.

Hybrid: an offspring of two different species that is often infertile.

Indusium: usually a thin scale-like membrane or structure covering the sorus.

Internode: that portion of a stem between two successive nodes.

Lanceolate: narrow, longer than wide and tapering at the end.

Lax: weak and appearing to droop as in the tip of some fronds.

Leptosporangiate: ferns with a thin-walled and stalked sporangium that unfurl from coiled fiddleheads.

Lobe: a distinct division or segment usually referring to the margin of a pinna or pinnule.

Lycosphen: a term once used to refer to the fern allies.

Margin: the edge of a pinna, for example.

Marginal: relating to the margin or edge of a leaf.

Megaspore: the larger of two types of spores found in quillworts and spikemosses; these spores produce female gametophytes.

Mesic: a moist and rich habitat.

Microspore: the smaller of two types of spores found in quillworts and spikemosses; these spores produce male gametophytes.

Midrib: the central, often raised axis of a frond, pinna or pinnule.

Mycorrhiza: symbiotic fungal association with higher plants.

Native: occurring naturally in the wild and not introduced by humans.

Node: that point on a stem where leaves or branches emerge.

Oblong: longer than wide with sides mostly parallel.

Opposite: form of growth in which leaves or stems arise in pairs at the nodes.

Outcrop: rocky projection often within a wooded area.

Ovate: egg-shaped.

Peduncle: the stalk supporting a cone or group of them found on the common clubmoss, for example.

Petiole: a leaf stalk sometimes referred to as a stipe in ferns.

Pinna: a distinct, primary division of the fern blade which can then be further divided into pinnules.

Pinnatifid: cut half to three-fourths to the rachis so that separate pinnae or pinnules are not formed.

Pinnule: the secondary pinna.

Pinnulet: the tertiary pinna cut into the pinnule.

Ploidy: number of chromosome sets in a cell; including haploid, diploid and tetraploid, for example.

Polyploidy: having more than two basic sets of chromosomes.

Prostrate: laying flat to the ground or substrate.

Prothallus: the tiny, sexual gametophyte stage of the plant; archegonium is female and antheridium is male.

Pteridologist: botanists proudly use this title in reference to those who study ferns as in, "Me? I am a pteridologist!"

Pteridophyte: the traditional, but underutilized, term encompassing all the plants in this field guide used by pteridologist as in, "watch your step, I see some beautiful pteridophytes over here!"

Rachis: the midrib of a compound frond bearing pinna.

Range: the geographic distribution of a species.

Reflexed: bent sharply downwards or backwards from attachment.

Revolute: rolled backward from the margins and turned under.

Rhizome: the woody parts of a rootstock often creeping just at the surface, as in the Interrupted Fern.

Rootstock: the short, erect stem arising from roots and bearing a frond.

Rugulose: covered with minute wrinkles.

Serrate: having sharp, saw-like teeth.

Sessile: without a stalk.

Siliceous: composed of or containing noticeable amounts of silica in some of the scouring rushes, for example.

Simple: undivided, not compound, usually in reference to a blade that is not divided to a midrib.

Sori: singular for sorus; so I said to the fern, "Aren't you a site for sori?"

Sorus: a cluster of spore cases or sporangia.

Spathulate: spatula or spoon-shaped.

Species: a group of organisms capable of interbreeding and having many characteristics in common.

Spike: an elongate and compact group of reproductive structures.

Spinulose: bearing small spines across a surface.

Sporangium: specialized structure in which spores are produced; also called a spore case.

Spore: a reproductive cell originating from the sporophyte that germinates into a prothallus of the gametophyte stage.

Sporophyll: a fertile leaf bearing sporangia.

Sporophyte: the obvious and familiar plant with roots, stems and leaves that produces spores during the species' life cycle.

Spreading: extending outward from the structure to which it is attached.

Sterile: in reference to the leaves that do not produce spore structures and the infertile hybrids.

Stipe: leaf stalk or petiole located at the base of a frond and attaching to the rootstock or rhizome.

Strobilus: a cone-shaped reproductive structure found in some club-mosses, for example.

Submersed: growing below the surface of water.

Subspecies: a subdivision of a species that is genetically unique.

Succulent: juicy and fleshy, as in some *Botrychium*.

Talus: rock debris deposited at the base of a cliff.

Taxonomy: scientific process of classifying and naming groups of organisms.

Terminal: at the end or apex of a structure.

Ternate: divided into 3 somewhat equal parts, as in Bracken Fern and Oak Fern.

Tetraploid: having four sets of chromosomes.

Toothed: having teeth long the margins of pinna, for example.

Tripinnate: a blade divided into pinnae, pinnules and then pinnulets, as in some wood ferns.

Triploid: having three sets of chromosomes.

Tropophore: the sterile blade of some ferns (*Botrychium*, for example) that does not produce reproductive structures.

Type species: the original species representative of a particular genus; for example, Common Clubmoss (*Lycopodium clavatum*) is the species that Linneaus determined represented the entire group of clubmosses.

Variety: plant having minor characters or variations that separates it from the type species.

Vascular: having specialized tissues (xylem and phloem) that conduct nutrients and other products throughout a plant.

Vein: vascular tissue visible within the plant leaf or pinna.

Velum: a thin membrane covering sporangium in quillworts, for example.

Whorl: three or more leaves arranged in a circle about an axis.

Winged: having a thin extension of tissue, for example along the rachis in some ferns.

Xeric: a very dry habitat.

Titles of Interest

Billington, Cecil. 1952. *Ferns of Michigan.* Cranbrook Institute of Science.

Chadde, Steve W. 2013. *Midwest Ferns: A Field Guide to the Ferns and Fern Relatives of the North Central United States.*

Cobb, Boughton, Cheryl Lowe and Elizabeth Farnsworth. 2005. *Peterson Field Guide to Ferns: Northeastern and Central North America, 2nd Edition.* New York Houghton Mifflin Company.

Flora of North America Editorial Committee (eds). 1993. *Flora of North America: North of Mexico Volume 2: Pteridophytes and Gymnosperms.* Oxford University Press. New York.

Hallowell, Anne C. and Barbara G. Hallowell. 2001. *Fern Finder: A Guide to Native Ferns of Central and Northeastern United States and Eastern Canada (Nature Study Guides).* Nature Study Guild Publishers. Rochester, New York.

Hoshizaki, Barbar J. and Robbin C. Moran. 2001. *Fern Grower's Manual: Revised and Expanded Edition.* Timber Press.

Lellinger, David B. 1985. *A Field Manual of the Ferns and Fern-Allies of the United States & Canada.* Smithsonian Institution Press. Washington, D.C.

Moran, Robbin C. 2004. *A Natural History of Ferns.* Timber Press.

Parsons, Frances T. 1961. *How to Know the Ferns and Fern Allies (The Pictured Key Nature Series).* Dover Publications, New York.

Ranker, Tom A. and Christopher H. Haufler. 2008. *Biology and Evolution of Ferns and Lycophytes.* Cambridge University Press.

Tryon, Rolla, N.C. Fassett, D.W. Dunlop and M.E. Diemer. 1940. *The Ferns and Fern Allies of Wisconsin.* University of Wisconsin.

Tryon, Rolla. 1980. *Ferns of Minnesota.* University of Minnesota Press.

Wherry, Edgar T. 1961. *The Fern Guide: Northeastern and Midland United States and Adjacent Canada.* Doubleday. New York.

Whittingham, Sarah. 2012. *Fern Fever: The Story of Pteridomania.* Frances Lincoln.

Fern Groups

American Fern Society

http://amerfernsoc.org/

The American Fern Society is over 100 years old. With over 900 members worldwide, it is one of the largest international fern clubs in the world. It was established in 1893 with the objective of fostering interest in ferns and fern allies.

Photo Credits

All photos are by the author except those listed below.

Donald Cameron: 75 bottom right, 91 bottom left

Flickr/Creative Commons License: 101 bottom (Homer Edward Price)

Jason Husveth/Creative Commons license: 69 bottom right, bottom middle, bottom left

Sparky Stensaas (www.ThePhotoNaturalist.com): front cover (all), 32, 35 middle left (crozier), bottom left, 111 middle center, middle left, 123 bottom left

Public Domain: 143 bottom

Sarah Waddle: 3 bottom

Wikimedia Commons/Creative Commons license: 45 bottom right, bottom left; 53 bottom (Luc Viatour); 64, 65, 67 top right, 75 (OpenCage), 93 bottom, 96, 97 (Muriel Bendel), 101 top (Tom Dorman), 115 bottom (Choess), 125 bottom left (Royce Milam), 128, 129 top (Choess), bottom left (Meneerke Bloem), bottom right (R. A. Nonemocher), 131 bottom (Muriel Bendel), 137 bottom left (Choess)

Appendix: Checklist and Naming

You probably already know that all plants and animals are given unique scientific names based on a binomial system (genus, species). These unique names show relationships. *Osmunda cinnamomea*, cinnamon fern, is clearly related to other *Osmunda* species. As we learn more about the organisms, names might change to show more accurate relationships. Recent genetic evidence clearly shows that cinnamon fern is actually a sister species to all other species in *Osmunda*. In response, taxonomists have suggested that *Osmundastrum cinnamomeum* might be an appropriate new name for cinnamon fern.

It can be very difficult to keep up with the changes. The list that follows contains information for naming of each species included in this field guide. Let's look more closely at ostrich fern.

A) Pg. 106 Ostrich Fern *Matteuccia struthiopteris*

B) *Matteuccia struthiopteris* var. *pensylvanica* (Willdenow) C. V. Morton, Amer. Fern J. 40: 247. 1950.

C) Shuttlecock Fern, Ostrich Plume Fern, Garden Fern

D) *Matteuccia pensylvanica, Pteretis pensylvanica*

Line A. The common and scientific names used in this guide are listed. Because they may not correspond with what you find in other resources, more information follows. On occasion, the scientific name differs from line B. In this case, variety *pensylvanica* was removed to simplify the name for print. A few times you will find an entirely different name that is in wide use but has not yet been officially accepted by the Flora of North America.

Line B. This is the official name used in the Flora of North America, Volume 2: Pteridophytes and Gymnosperms, published in 1993. Following the scientific name is a wealth of information. You can see that this name was first published in 1950 in the American Fern Journal, edition 40 on page 247. Conrad Vernon Morton (1905-1972) was an American botanist who worked extensively on ferns. His work built upon the work of Carl Ludwig Willdenow (1765-1812), a German botanist and plant taxonomist. Willdenow named this species *Struthiopteris pensylvanica* in 1810. Morton retained parts of the old name while describing a new genus and labeling this as variety *pensylvanica*.

Line C. Common names are quite varied and interesting in their own right. Often, they highlight cultural uses (garden fern) or obvious visual characteristics (ostrich plume fern). Only a few of the most interesting names are included.

Line D. Finally, a few other scientific names are listed. When you reference other field guides or local floras, you will routinely find some of these other older or newer names used. You will notice four related, but unique, scientific names for Ostrich Fern. I have found 14 names that have been used over time, but only included a few examples for this species.

Next to each unique collection of names you will find a box. As you observe new species, check them off here to keep your records organized and accessible. You will also see the page number corresponding to the species description.

❏ Pg. 28 Common Clubmoss *Lycopodium clavatum*
Lycopodium clavatum Linnaeus, Sp. Pl. 2: 1101. 1753.
Stag's Horn Clubmoss, Running-pine

❏ Pg. 28 One-cone Clubmoss *Lycopodium lagopus*
Lycopodium lagopus (Laestadius ex C. Hartman) G. Zinserling ex Kuzeneva Prochorova, Fl. Murmansk. Obl. 1: 80. 1953.
One-cone Ground-pine
Lycopodium clavatum subsp *megastachyon*

❑ **Pg. 30 Bristly Clubmoss** *Spinulum annotinum*
Lycopodium annotinum Linnaeus, Sp. Pl. 2: 1103. 1753.
Stiff Clubmoss, Interrupted Clubmoss
Lycopodium dubium

❑ **Pg. 32 Bog Clubmoss** *Lycopodiella inundata*
Lycopodiella inundata (Linnaeus) Holub, Preslia. 36: 21. 1964.
Inundated Clubmoss, Northern Bog Clubmoss
Lepidotis inundata

❑ **Pg. 34 Shining Firmoss** *Huperzia lucidula*
Huperzia lucidula (Michaux) Trevisan, Atti Soc. Ital. Sci. Nat. 17: 248. 1875.
Shining Clubmoss
Huperzia selago susp *lucidula*

❑ **Pg. 34 Rock Firmoss** *Huperzia porophila*
Huperzia porophila (F. E. Lloyd & L. Underwood) Holub, Folia Geobot. Phytotax. 20: 76. 1985.
Lycopodium lucidulum var *porophilum*

❑ **Pg. 36 Northern Firmoss** *Huperzia selago*
Huperzia selago (Linnaeus) Bernhardi ex Schrank & Martius, Hort. Reg. Monac. 3. 1829.
Mountain Clubmoss, Fir-moss
Lycopodium selago

❑ **Pg. 36 Mountain Firmoss** *Huperzia appalachiana*
Huperzia appalachiana Beitel & Mickel, Amer. Fern J. 82: 42. 1992.
Appalachian Clubmoss
Huperzia appressa

❑ **Pg. 38 Prickly Tree Clubmoss** *Dendrolycopodium dendroideum*
Lycopodium dendroideum Michaux, Fl. Bor.-Amer. 2: 282. 1803.
Tree Groundpine
Lycopodium obscurum var *dendroideum*

❑ **Pg. 38 Flat-branched Tree Clubmoss** *Dendrolycopodium obscurum*
Lycopodium obscurum Linnaeus, Sp. Pl. 2: 1102. 1753.
Rare Clubmoss, Princess-pine

❑ **Pg. 38 Hickey's Tree Clubmoss** *Dendrolycopodium hickeyi*
Lycopodium hickeyi W. H. Wagner, Beitel, & R. C. Moran , Amer. Fern J. 79: 119--121. 1989.
Pennsylvania Clubmoss, Hickey's Clubmoss
Lycopodium obscurum var *isophyllum*

❑ **Pg. 40 Northern Ground Cedar** *Diphasiastrum complanatum*
Diphasiastrum complanatum (Linnaeus) Holub, Preslia. 47: 108. 1975.
Flat-stemmed Groundpine, Creeping Jenny, Christmas Green
Lycopodium complanatum

❑ **Pg. 40 Southern Ground Cedar** *Diphasiastrum digitatum*
Diphasiastrum digitatum (Dillenius ex A. Braun) Holub, Preslia. 47: 108. 1975.
Fan Clubmoss, Fan Creeping-cedar
Lycopodium digitatum, Lycopodium flabelliforme

❑ **Pg. 40 Blue Ground Cedar** *Diphasiastrum tristachyum*
Diphasiastrum tristachyum (Pursh) Holub, Preslia. 47: 108. 1975.
Deeproot Clubmoss, Deep-root Creeping-cedar
Lycopodium tristachyum

☐ **Pg. 44 Rock Spikemoss** *Selaginella rupestris*
Selaginella rupestris (Linnaeus) Spring, Flora. 21: 182. 1838.
Dwarf Spikemoss, Ledge Spikemoss, Sand Clubmoss, Festoon Pine
Lycopodium rupestre

☐ **Pg. 44 Northern Spikemoss** *Selaginella selaginoides*
Selaginella selaginoides (Linnaeus) Palisot de Beauvois ex Martius & Schrank, Hort.
Reg. Monac. 1: 182. 1829.
Club Spikemoss. Low Spikemoss
Selaginella ciliata

☐ **Pg. 46 Braun's Quillwort** *Isoëtes echinospora*
Isoëtes echinospora Durieu, Bull. Soc. Bot. France. 8:164. 1861.
Stiff Quillwort, Spiny-spore Quillwort
Isoetes braunii

☐ **Pg. 46 Lake Quillwort** *Isoëtes lacustris*
Isoëtes lacustris Linnaeus, Sp. Pl. 2: 1100. 1753.
Western Lake Quillwort
Isoëtes macrospora

☐ **Pg. 50 Field Horsetail** *Equisetum arvense*
Equisetum arvense Linnaeus, Sp. Pl. 2: 1061. 1753.
Common Horsetail, Western Horsetail
Equisetum calderi

☐ **Pg. 50 Meadow Horsetail** *Equisetum pratense*
Equisetum pratense Ehrhart, Hannover. Mag. 22: 138. 1784.
Shady Horsetail
Equisetum umbrosum

☐ **Pg. 52 Water Horsetail** *Equisetum fluviatile*
Equisetum fluviatile Linnaeus, Sp. Pl. 2: 1062. 1753.
River Horsetail, Pipes, Great Horsetail
Equisetum limosum

☐ **Pg. 52 Marsh Horsetail** *Equisetum palustre*
Equisetum palustre Linnaeus, Sp. Pl. 2: 1061. 1753.
Equisetum palustre var. *americanum*

☐ **Pg. 54 Wood Horsetail** *Equisetum sylvaticum*
Equisetum sylvaticum Linnaeus, Sp. Pl. 2: 1061. 1753.
Woodland Horsetail
Equisetum sylvaticum var. *multiramosum*

☐ **Pg. 56 Tall Scouring Rush** *Equisetum hyemale*
Equisetum hyemale subsp. *affine* (Engelmann) Calder & Roy L. Taylor, Canad. J.
Bot. 43: 1387. 1965.
Rough Horsetail, Dutch Rush, Shave-grass, Common Scouring Rush
Hippochaete hyemalis

☐ **Pg. 56 Smooth Horsetail** *Equisetum laevigatum*
Equisetum laevigatum A. Braun, Amer. J. Sci. Arts. 46: 87. 1844.
Smooth Scouring Rush
Equisetum funstonii, Hippochaete laevigata

☐ **Pg. 58 Variegated Scouring Rush** *Equisetum variegatum*
Equisetum variegatum Schleicher ex F. Weber & D. Mohr, Bot. Taschenb. 60, 447.
1807.
Variegated Horsetail
Hippochaete variegata

❏ **Pg. 60 Dwarf Scouring Rush** *Equisetum scirpoides*
Equisetum scirpoides Michaux, Fl. Bor.-Amer. 2: 281. 1803.
Dwarf Horsetail, Sedge Horsetail
Equisetum hyemale var. *tenellum, Hippochaete scirpoides*

❏ **Pg. 64 Northern Adder's Tongue** *Ophioglossum pusillum*
Ophioglossum pusillum Rafinesque, Précis Découv. Somiol. 46. 1814.
Northern Adder's Tongue Fern
Ophioglossum vulgatum

❏ **Pg. 66 Common Moonwort** *Botrychium lunaria*
Botrychium lunaria (Linnaeus) Swartz, J. Bot. (Schrader). 1800(2): 110. 1801.
Moonwort Grapefern
Botrychium onondagense

❏ **Pg. 68 Least Moonwort** *Botrychium simplex*
Botrychium simplex E. Hitchcock, Amer. J. Sci. 6: 103, plate 8. 1823.
Dwarf Grapefern, Simple Moonwort
Botrychium tenebrosum

❏ **Pg. 68 Little Goblin Moonwort** *Botrychium mormo*
Botrychium mormo W. H. Wagner, Amer. Fern J. 71: 26. 1981.

❏ **Pg. 70 Pale Moonwort** *Botrychium pallidum*
Botrychium pallidum W. H. Wagner, Amer. Fern J. 80: 74. 1990.
Pale Botrychium

❏ **Pg. 70 Prairie Moonwort** *Botrychium campestre*
Botrychium campestre W. H. Wagner & Farrar, Amer. Fern J. 76: 39, figs. 2, 4, 5.
1986.
Iowa Moonwort

❏ **Pg. 70 Mingan Moonwort** *Botrychium minganense*
Botrychium minganense Victorin, Proc. & Trans. Roy. Soc. Canada. ser. 3, 21: 331.
1927.
Mingan Island Grapefern
Botrychium lunaria subsp *minganense*

❏ **Pg. 70 Spoon-leaf Moonwort** *Botrychium spathulatum*
Botrychium spathulatum W. H. Wagner, Amer. Fern J. 80: 77. 1990.
Spatulate Moonwort

❏ **Pg. 72 Daisy-leaf Moonwort** *Botrychium matricariifolium*
Botrychium matricariifolium (Döll) A. Braun ex W. D. J. Koch, Syn. Deut. Schweiz.
Fl., ed. 2. 7: 1009. 1847.
Matricaria-leaved Grapefern, Chamomile Grapefern

❏ **Pg. 72 Triangle Moonwort** *Botrychium lanceolatum*
Botrychium lanceolatum (S. G. Gmelin) Angström, Bot. Not. 1854: 68. 1854.
Lance-leaved Grapefern
Botrychium angustisegmentum

❏ **Pg. 74 Leathery Grapefern** *Botrychium multifidum*
Botrychium multifidum (S. G. Gmelin) Ruprecht, Bemerk. Botrychium. 40. 1859.
Northern Grapefern,
Sceptridium multifidum

❏ **Pg. 74 Blunt-lobed Grapefern** *Botrychium oneidense*
Botrychium oneidense (Gilbert) House, Amer. Midl. Naturalist. 7: 126. 1905.
Botrychium multifidum var *oneidense*

❏ **Pg. 74 Rugulose Grapefern** *Botrychium rugulosum*
Botrychium rugulosum W. H. Wagner, Contr. Univ. Michigan Herb. 15: 315. 1982.
Ternate Grapefern
Sceptridium rugulosum

❏ **Pg. 76 Dissected Grapefern** *Botrychium dissectum*
Botrychium dissectum Sprengel, Anleit. Kenntn. Gew. 3: 172. 1804.
Bronze Fern, Cutleaf Grapefern
Sceptridium dissectum

❏ **Pg. 78 Rattlesnake Fern** *Botrychium virginianum*
Botrychium virginianum (Linnaeus) Swartz, J. Bot. (Schrader). 1800(2): 111. 1801.
Rattlesnake Grapefern
Botrypus virginianus

❏ **Pg. 82 Eastern Bracken Fern** *Pteridium aquilinum*
Pteridium aquilinum var. *latiusculum* (Desvaux) L. Underwood ex A. Heller, Cat. N.
Amer. Pl. ed. 3. 17. 1909.
Eastern Bracken, Bracken Fern, Northern Bracken Fern, Eagle Fern
Pteris aquilina

❏ **Pg. 84 Northern Maidenhair Fern** *Adiantum pedatum*
Adiantum pedatum Linnaeus, Sp. Pl. 2: 1095. 1753.
Maidenfern
Adiantum boreale

❏ **Pg. 86 Interrupted Fern** *Osmunda claytoniana*
Osmunda claytoniana Linnaeus, Sp. Pl. 2: 1066. 1753.
Clayton's Fern
Osmunda claytoniana subsp. *pilosa*

❏ **Pg. 88 Northern Lady Fern** *Athyrium filix-femina*
Athyrium filix-femina var. *angustum* (Willdenow) G. Lawson, Edinburgh New Philos.
J. n.s. 19: 115. 1864.
Ladyfern, Subarctic Ladyfern, Common Ladyfern
Athyrium angustum

❏ **Pg. 90 Silvery Spleenwort** *Deparia acrostichoides*
Deparia acrostichoides (Swartz) M. Kato, Ann. Carnegie Mus. 49: 177. 1980.
Silver False Spleenwort, Silvery Glade Fern
Athyrium thelypteroides, Diplazium acrostichoides

❏ **Pg. 92 New York Fern** *Thelypteris noveboracensis*
Thelypteris noveboracensis (Linnaeus) Nieuwland, Amer. Midl. Naturalist. 1: 225.
1910.
Tapering Fern
Parathelypteris noveboracensis, Dryopteris noveboracensis

❏ **Pg. 94 Spinulose Wood Fern** *Dryopteris carthusiana*
Dryopteris carthusiana (Villars) H. P. Fuchs, Bull. Soc. Bot. France. 105: 339. 1959.
Toothed Woodfern
Dryopteris spinulosa

❏ **Pg. 94 Northern Wood Fern** *Dryopteris expansa*
Dryopteris expansa (C. Presl) Fraser Jenkins & Jermy, Brit. Fern Gaz. 11: 338. 1977.
Spreading Woodfern
Dryopteris spinulosa var *dilatata*

❏ **Pg. 96 Male Fern** *Dryopteris filix-mas*
Dryopteris filix-mas (Linnaeus) Schott, Gen. Fil. plate 67. 1834.
Thelypteris filix-mas

❏ **Pg. 98 Evergreen Wood Fern** *Dryopteris intermedia*
Dryopteris intermedia (Muhlenberg ex Willdenow) A. Gray, Manual. 630. 1848.
Intermediate Woodfern, Fancy Fern
Dryopteris spinulosa var *intermedia*

❏ **Pg. 100 Marginal Wood Fern** *Dryopteris marginalis*
Dryopteris marginalis (Linnaeus) A. Gray, Manual. 632. 1848.
Marginal Shield Fern
Microlepia marginata var. *marginata*

❏ **Pg. 102 Common Oak Fern** *Gymnocarpium dryopteris*
Gymnocarpium dryopteris (Linnaeus) Newman, Phytologist. 4: app. 24. 1851.
Northern Oak Fern, Oak Fern
Dryopteris dryopteris, Phegopteris dryopteris

❏ **Pg. 102 Nahanni Oak Fern** *Gymnocarpium jessoense*
Gymnocarpium jessoense subsp. *parvulum* Sarvela, Ann. Bot. Fenn. 15: 103. 1978.
Asian Oakfern, Northern Oak Fern

❏ **Pg. 102 Limestone Oak Fern** *Gymnocarpium robertianum*
Gymnocarpium robertianum (Hoffman) Newman, Phytologist. 4: app. 24. 1851.
Limestone Fern, Scented Oak Fern
Dryopteris robertiana, Phegopteris robertiana

❏ **Pg. 104 Northern Beech Fern** *Phegopteris connectilis*
Phegopteris connectilis (Michaux) Watt, Canad. Naturalist & Quart. J. Sci. 3: 29. 1866.
Long Beech Fern, Narrow Beech Fern
Thelypteris phegopteris, Phegopteris polypodioides

❏ **Pg. 104 Broad Beech Fern** *Phegopteris hexagonoptera*
Phegopteris hexagonoptera (Michaux) Fée, 5: 242. 1852.
Southern Beech Fern
Dryopteris hexagonoptera

❏ **Pg. 106 Ostrich Fern** *Matteuccia struthiopteris*
Matteuccia struthiopteris var. *pensylvanica* (Willdenow) C. V. Morton, Amer. Fern J. 40: 247. 1950.
Shuttlecock Fern, Ostrich Plume Fern, Garden Fern
Matteuccia pensylvanica, Pteretis pensylvanica

❏ **Pg. 108 Bead Fern** *Onoclea sensibilis*
Onoclea sensibilis Linnaeus, Sp. Pl. 2: 1062. 1753.
Sensitive Fern
Onoclea sensibilis var. *obtusilobata*

❏ **Pg. 110 Cinnamon Fern** *Osmunda cinnamomea*
Osmunda cinnamomea Linnaeus, Sp. Pl. 2: 1066. 1753.
Osmundastrum cinnamomeum, Struthiopteris cinnamomea

❏ **Pg. 112 Royal Fern** *Osmunda regalis*
Osmunda regalis var. *spectabilis* (Willdenow) A. Gray, Manual ed. 2. 600. 1856.
American Royal Fern, Flowering Fern
Osmunda spectabilis, Struthiopteris regalis

❑ **Pg. 114 Goldie's Wood Fern** *Dryopteris goldiana*
Dryopteris goldiana (Hooker ex Goldie) A. Gray, Manual. 631. 1848.
Goldie's Fern
Thelypteris goldiana

❑ **Pg. 116 Crested Wood Fern** *Dryopteris cristata*
Dryopteris cristata (Linnaeus) A. Gray, Manual. 631. 1848.
Crested Shieldfern
Polypodium cristatum

❑ **Pg. 118 Northern Marsh Fern** *Thelypteris palustris*
Thelypteris palustris var. *pubescens* (Lawson) Fernald, Rhodora. 31: 34. 1929.
Eastern Marsh Fern, Meadow Fern
Dryopteris thelypteris

❑ **Pg. 120 Braun's Holly Fern** *Polystichum braunii*
Polystichum braunii (Spenner) Fée, 5: 278. 1852.
Eastern Holly Fern
Polystichum braunii subsp. *purshii*

❑ **Pg. 120 Northern Holly Fern** *Polystichum lonchitis*
Polystichum lonchitis (Linnaeus) Roth, Tent. Fl. Germ. 3(1): 71. 1799.
Narrow Holly Fern
Polystichum mohrioides var *lemmonii*

❑ **Pg. 122 Rock Polypody** *Polypodium virginianum*
Polypodium virginianum Linnaeus, Sp. Pl. 2: 1085. 1753.
Common Polypody, Rock-cap Fern
Polypodium vulgare var *virginianum*

❑ **Pg. 124 Smooth Cliff Brake** *Pellaea glabella*
Pellaea glabella Mettenius ex Kuhn, Linnaea. 36: 87. 1869.
Slender Cliff Brake
Pellaea atropurpurea var *bushii*

❑ **Pg. 124 Purple-stem Cliff Brake** *Pellaea atropurpurea*
Pellaea atropurpurea (Linnaeus) Link, Fil. Spec. 59. 1841.
Purple Cliffbrake
Allosorus atropurpureus

❑ **Pg. 126 Slender Cliff Brake** *Cryptogramma stelleri*
Cryptogramma stelleri (S. G. Gmelin) Prantl in Engler, Bot. Jahrb. Syst. 3: 413. 1882.
Fragile Rock Brake, Steller's Rock Brake
Allosorus gracilis

❑ **Pg. 128 Walking Fern** *Asplenium rhizophyllum*
Asplenium rhizophyllum Linnaeus, Sp. Pl. 2: 1078. 1753.
Walking Fern Spleenwort
Camptosorus rhizophyllus

❑ **Pg. 128 American Hart's-tongue Fern** *Asplenium scolopendrium*
Asplenium scolopendrium var. *americanum* (Fernald) Kartesz & Gandhi, Phytologia. 70: 196. 1991.
Hart's-tongue Fern
Phyllitis scolopendrium var *americana*

❑ **Pg. 130 Maidenhair Spleenwort** *Asplenium trichomanes*
Asplenium trichomanes Linnaeus, Sp. Pl. 2: 1080. 1753.
Common Maidenhair
Asplenium melanocaulon

❏ **Pg. 130 Green Spleenwort** *Asplenium viride*
Asplenium trichomanes-ramosum Linnaeus, Sp. Pl. 2: 1082. 1753.
Bright-green Spleenwort

❏ **Pg. 132 Fragrant Fern** *Dryopteris fragrans*
Dryopteris fragrans (Linnaeus) Schott, Gen. Fil. plate 9. 1834.
Fragrant Woodfern
Thelypteris fragrans

❏ **Pg. 134 Bulblet Bladderfern** *Cystopteris bulbifera*
Cystopteris bulbifera (Linnaeus) Bernhardi, Neues J. Bot. 1(2): 10. 1806.
Bulblet Fern
Filix bulbifera

❏ **Pg. 134 Laurentian Bladderfern** *Cystopteris laurentiana*
Cystopteris laurentiana (Weatherby) Blasdell, Mem. Torrey Bot. Club. 21(4): 51. 1963.
St Lawrence Bladder Fern
Cystopteris fragilis var *laurentiana*

❏ **Pg. 136 Fragile Fern** *Cystopteris fragilis*
Cystopteris fragilis (Linnaeus) Bernhardi, Neues J. Bot. 1(2): 26, plate 2, fig. 9. 1806.
Brittle Bladder Fern
Filix fragilis

❏ **Pg. 136 Mackay's Fragile Bladderfern** *Cystopteris tenuis*
Cystopteris tenuis (Michaux) Desvaux, 6: 264. 1827.
Brittle Bladder Fern, Upland Brittle Fern
Cystopteris fragilis var *mackayi*

❏ **Pg. 138 Smooth Cliff Fern** *Woodsia glabella*
Woodsia glabella R. Brown ex Richardson in Franklin, Narr. Journey Polar Sea. 754. 1823.
Smooth Woodsia
Woodsia alpina var. *glabella*

❏ **Pg. 138 Alpine Cliff Fern** *Woodsia alpina*
Woodsia alpina (Bolton) Gray, Nat. Arr. Brit. Pl. 2: 17. 1821.
Alpine Woodsia, Northern Woodsia
Woodsia glabella var *bellii*

❏ **Pg. 140 Rusty Cliff Fern** *Woodsia ilvensis*
Woodsia ilvensis (Linnaeus) R. Brown, Trans. Linn. Soc. London, Bot. 11: 173. 1813.
Rusty Woodsia, Oblong Woodsia
Acrostichum ilvense

❏ **Pg. 142 Oregon Cliff Fern** *Woodsia oregana*
Woodsia oregana D. C. Eaton, Canad. Naturalist & Quart. J. Sci. n. s. 2: 90. 1865.
Oregon Woodsia
Woodsia cathcartiana

❏ **Pg. 142 Rocky Mountain Cliff Fern** *Woodsia scopulina*
Woodsia scopulina D. C. Eaton, Canad. Naturalist & Quart. J. Sci. 2: 91. 1865.
Rocky Mountain Woodsia
Woodsia obtusa var. *lyallii*

Index

ABC

Adder's Tongue, Northern 64
Adiantum pedatum 84
Africa 112
Alpine Cliff Fern 138
Alzheimer's Disease 34
angiosperms 11
ant 64
antheridia 13
apogamy 15
archegonia 13
Asia 112
Asplenium 17
Asplenium rhizophyllum 128
Asplenium trichomanes 130
Asplenium viride 130
Athyrium filix-femina 88
Bead Fern 14, 18, 108
Beech Fern,
—Broad 104
—Northern 15, 104
Bladder Fern,
—Bulblet 15, 134
—Laurentian 134
Blue Ground Cedar 40
Blunt-lobed Grapefern 74
Bog Clubmoss 16, 32
Botrychium 14, 18
Botrychium campestre 70
Botrychium dissectum 76
Botrychium lanceolatum 72
Botrychium lunaria 66
Botrychium matricariifolium 72
Botrychium minganese 70
Botrychium mormo 68
Botrychium multifidum 74
Botrychium oneidense 74
Botrychium pallidum 70
Botrychium rugulosum 74
Botrychium simplex 68
Botrychium spathulatum 70
Botrychium virginianum 78
Bracken Fern 3, 5, 15
—Eastern 82
Braun, Alexander 120
Braun's Holly Fern 80, 120
Braun's Quillwort 46
Bristly Clubmoss 30
Broad Beech Fern 104
Bulblet Bladder Fern 15, 134
Calamites 5, 8
Carboniferous Period 6, 8
China 4
chlorophyllous tissue 49
Christmas decorations 40
Cinnamon Fern 5, 9, 11, 16, 22, 110
circinate vernation 22
Cliff Brake,
—Purple Stem 124
—Slender 126
—Smooth 15, 124

Cliff Fern,
—Alpine 138
—Mountain 142
—Oregon 142
—Rusty 140
—Smooth 138
climate change 5
Clinton's Wood Fern 114
Clubmoss,
—Bog 16, 32
—Bristly 30
—Common 28
—Flat-branched Tree 38
—Hickey's Tree 38
—One-cone 28
—Prickly Tree 38
clubmosses 6
Common Clubmoss 28
Common Moonwort 66
Common Oak Fern 102
Common Polypody 5, 19, 122
Costa Rica 4
Crested Wood Fern 116
Cretaceous Period 5, 11
croziers 22
Cryptogramma stelleri 126
Cut-leaved Grapefern 76
Cystoperis fragilis 136
Cystopteris bulbifera 134
Cystopteris laurentiana 134
Cystopteris tenuis 136

DE

Daisy-leaf Moonwort 72
Dendrolycopodium dendroideum 38
Dendrolycopodium hickeyi 38
Dendrolycopodium obscurum 38
Dennstaedtia punctilobula 92
Deparia acrostichoides 90
Devonian Period 9
dinosaurs 11, 86
Diphasiastrum 15
Diphasiastrum complanatum 40
Diphasiastrum digitatum 40
Diphasiastrum tristachyum 40
diploid 15
Dissected Grapefern 76
Doctrine of Signatures 2, 84
dragonflies, giant 9
Dryopteris carthusiana 94
Dryopteris clintoniana 114
Dryopteris cristata 116
Dryopteris expansa 94
Dryopteris filix-mas 96
Dryopteris fragrans 132
Dryopteris goldiana 114
Dryopteris intermedia 98
Dryopteris marginalis 100
Dwarf Scouring Rush 60
earthworms 68
Eastern Bracken Fern 82
Equisetum 15
Equisetum arvense 50

Equisetum fluviatile 52
Equisetum hyemale 56
Equisetum laevigatum 56
Equisetum palustre 54
Equisetum pratense 50
Equisetum scirpoides 60
Equisetum sylvaticum 54
Equisetum variegatum 58
Estonia 140
Europe 4, 112
Eusporangiate ferns 7
Evergreen Wood Fern 17, 18, 98

F

Fagitana littera 118
fern fever 1
fern uses,
—eating 3
—sandpaper 3
Fern,
—Alpine Cliff 138
—Bead 14, 18, 108
—Bracken 3, 5, 15
—Braun's Holly 80, 120
—Broad Beech 104
—Bulblet Bladder 15, 134
—Cinnamon 5, 9, 11, 16, 22, 110
—Clinton's Wood 114
—Common Oak 102
—Crested Wood 116
—Eastern Bracken 82
—Evergreen Wood 17, 18, 98
—Fragile 136
—Fragrant 132
—Goldie's Wood 114
—Hay-scented 92
—Holly 120
—Interrupted 11, 86
—Lady 5
—Laurentian Bladder 134
—Limestone Oak 102
—Mackay's Brittle 136
—Maidenhair 3
—Male 96
—Marginal Wood 14, 100
—Mountain Cliff 142
—Nahanni Oak 102
—New York 92
—Northern Beech 15, 104
—Northern Lady 88
—Northern Maidenhair 17, 84
—Northern Marsh 16, 118
—Northern Wood 94
—Oak 5
—Oregon Cliff 142
—Ostrich 3, 14, 22, 106
—Rattlesnake 78
—Royal 11, 16, 80, 112
—Rusty Cliff 18, 140
—Sensitive 14, 18. 108
—Silvery Glade 90
—Smooth Cliff 138

—Spinulose Wood 94
—Walking 128
ferns,
—and logging 104
—and rock climbing 136
—basketry 84
—carcinogen 22
—disturbed areas 16
—edible 106
—finding 16
—forests 16
—life cycle 12
—lore of invisibility 96
—medical uses 116
—medical uses 130
—orchid propagation 110
—reproduction 12
—rocky outcrops 16
—seasons 17-18
—wet areas 16
fertile frond 14
fertilization 13
fiddleheads 17, 18, 22-26
Field Horsetail 18, 50
Firmoss,
—Mountain 36
—Northern 36
—Rock 34
—Shining 34
Flat-branched Tree Clubmoss 38
Fragile Fern 136
Fragrant Fern 132
fungus, White Rot 8

GHI

gametophyte 13
gemmae 15
genetically modified organism 11
Glomus 70
GMO 11
Goldie, John 114
Goldie's Wood Fern 114
Gondwanaland 9
Good, Ronald 2
Grapefern,
—Blunt-lobed 76
—Blunt-lobed 74
—Cut-leaved 76
—Leathery 74
—Rugulose 74
Green Spleenwort 130
Ground Cedar,
—Blue 40
—Northern 40
—Southern 40
Gymnocarpium dryopteris 102
Gymnocarpium jessoense 102
Gymnocarpium robertianum 102
gymnosperms 11
haploid 12
Hay-scented Fern 92
Hickey's Tree Clubmoss 38

Holly Fern 120
—Braun's 80, 120
—Northern 120
Homo sapiens 86
hornwort 11
Horsetail,
—Field 18, 50
—Forest 3
—Marsh 54
—Meadow 50
—River 52
—Water 16, 52
—Wood 54
horsetails 5, 7, 48
Huperzia 15, 17
Huperzia appressa 36
Huperzia lucidula 34
Huperzia porophila 34
Huperzia selago 36
huperzine 34
hybridization 15
indusium 102
Interrupted Fern 11, 86
Isoetes echinospora 46
Isoetes lacustris 46

JKL
Jack Pine 74
Jurassic Period 5
Lady Fern 5
—Northern 88
Lake Quillwort 46
Laurasia 9
Laurentian Bladder Fern 134
Least Moonwort 68
Leathery Grapefern 74
leptosporangiate ferns 7
Little Goblin Moonwort 17, 68
lycophytes 6
Lycopodiella inundata 32
Lycopodium annotinum 30
Lycopodium clavatum 28
Lycopodium dendroideum 38
Lycopodium inundata 32
Lycopodium lagopus 28
Lycopodium lucidula 34
Lycopodium selago 36

MNO
Mackay's Brittle Fern 136
Maidenhair Fern 3
—Northern 17, 84
Maidenhair Spleenwort 81, 130
Male Fern 96
Marginal Wood Fern 14, 100
Marsh Fern Moth 118
Marsh Fern,
—Northern 16, 118
Marsh Horsetail 54
Matteuccia struthiopteris 106
Meadow Horsetail 50
megaspores 16

microspores 16
Mingan Moonwort 70
moonwort anatomy 63
Moonwort,
—Common 66
—Daisy-leaf 72
—Least 68
—Little Goblin 17, 68
—Mingan 70
—Pale 70
—Prairie 15, 70
—Spoon-leaf 70
—Triangle 72
moonworts 62
moss 44
Moth, Marsh Fern 118
Mountain Cliff Fern 142
Mountain Firmoss 36
Muskrat 52
mycorrhizal fungi 15
Myrmecia pilosula 64
Nahanni Oak Fern 102
neochrome 11
New York Fern 92
Niagara Escarpment 128
Norse mythology 110
Northern Adder's Tongue 64
Northern Beech Fern 104
Northern Beech Fern 15
Northern Firmoss 36
Northern Ground Cedar 40
Northern Lady Fern 88
Northern Maidenhair Fern 17, 84
Northern Marsh Fern 118
Northern Spikemoss 44
Northern Wood Fern 94
Oak Fern 5
—Common 102
—Limestone 102
—Nahanni 102
One-cone Clubmoss 28
Onoclea sensibilis 108
Ophioglossum pusillum 64
Oregon Cliff Fern 142
Osmunda cinnamomea 5, 110
Osmunda claytoniana 86
Osmunda regalis 112
Osmunder 110
Ostrich Fern 14, 22, 106

PQR
Pale Moonwort 70
Pangea 5
Pellaea 17
Pellaea atropurpurea 124
Pellaea glabella 124
Permian Period 5
Phegopteris connectilis 104
Phegopteris hexagonoptera 104
Pine,
—Jack 74
—Red 74

Polypodium virginianum 122
Polypody,
—Common 5, 19, 122
—Rock 122
Polystichum braunii 120
Polystichum lonchitis 120
Polytrichum 44
Prairie Moonwort 15, 70
Prickly Tree Clubmoss 38
prothallus 13
ptaquiloside 22
Pteridium aquilinum 82
pteridomania 1
Purple Stem Cliff Brake 124
Quillwort,
—Braun's 46
—Lake 46
quillworts 7, 43
Rattlesnake Fern 78
Red Pine 74
reproduction 12
—vegetative 15
rhizome 15
River Horsetail 52
Rock Firmoss 34
Rock Polypody 122
Rock Spikemoss 44
Rock-cap Fern 122
Royal Fern 11, 16, 80, 112
Rugulose Grapefern 74
Rusty Cliff Fern 18, 140

ST

sandpaper substitute 56
Scouring Rush,
—Dwarf 60
—Smooth 56
—Tall 56
—Variegated 58
scouring rushes 5
Selaginella rupestris 44
Selaginella selaginoides 44
Sensitive Fern 14, 18, 108
Shakespeare 2
Shining Firmoss 34
silica 56
Silvery Glade Fern 90
Silvery Spleenwort 90
Slender Cliff Brake 126
Smooth Cliff Brake 15, 124
Smooth Cliff Fern 138
Smooth Scouring Rush 56
South America 112
Southern Ground Cedar 40
sperm 13
Spikemoss,
—Northern 44
—Rock 44
spikemosses 6, 42
Spinulose Wood Fern 94
Spinulum annotinum 30
Spleenwort 5

—Green 130
—Maidenhair 81, 130
—Silvery 90
Spoon-leaf Moonwort 70
sporangia 14
spore dispersal 14
spores 12
sporophyte 13, 14
Staghorn Sumac 74
Steller, George Wilhelm 126
sterile frond 14
Sumac, Staghorn 74
Tall Scouring Rush 56
tetraploid 15
Thelypteris noveboracensis 92
Thelypteris palustris 118
Thor 110
Thoreau, Henry David 19
Triangle Moonwort 72
Triassic Period 5
triploid 15
typical ferns 80

UVW

Variegated Scouring Rush 58
violin maker 3, 56
Wagner, Warren and Florence 64
Walking Fern 128
Ward, Dr. Nathaniel 4
Wardian Case 4
Water Horsetail 16, 52
Wherry, Edgar 16
White Rot fungus 8
Wood Fern,
—Clinton's 114
—Crested 116
—Evergreen 17, 18, 98
—Goldie's 114
—Marginal 14, 100
—Northern 94
—Spinulose 94
Wood Horsetail 54
Woods, Joseph 138
Woodsia 81
Woodsia alpina 138
Woodsia glabella 138
Woodsia ilvensis 140
Woodsia oregona 142
Woodsia scopulina 142
worms 68

Field Notes

Field Notes

Field Notes

Field Notes

Other user-friendly field guides from
Kollath-Stensaas Publishing

Fascinating Fungi of the North Woods
Cora Mollen & Larry Weber

Wildflowers of the BWCA & North Shore
Mark Sparky Stensaas

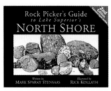

Rock Picker's Guide to Lake Superior's North Shore
Mark Sparky Stensaas

Amazing Agates: Lake Superior's Banded Gemstone
Scott Wolter

Orchids of the North Woods
Kim & Cindy Risen

Mammals of the North Woods
Roger and Consie Powell

Insects of the North Woods
Jeff Hahn

Moths of the North Woods
Jim Sogaard

Dragonflies of the North Woods
Kurt Mead

Lichens of the North Woods
Joe Walewski

Spiders of the North Woods
Larry Weber

Butterflies of the North Woods
Larry Weber

more at www.kollathstensaas.com